The Non-financial Manager's Guide to Business Decision Making

Understanding and Integrating the Roles of Accounting, Finance and Controlling

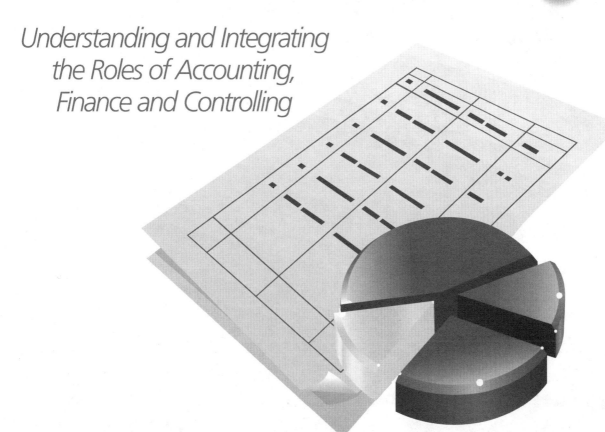

The Non-financial Manager's Guide to
Business Decision Making

*Understanding and Integrating
the Roles of Accounting,
Finance and Controlling*

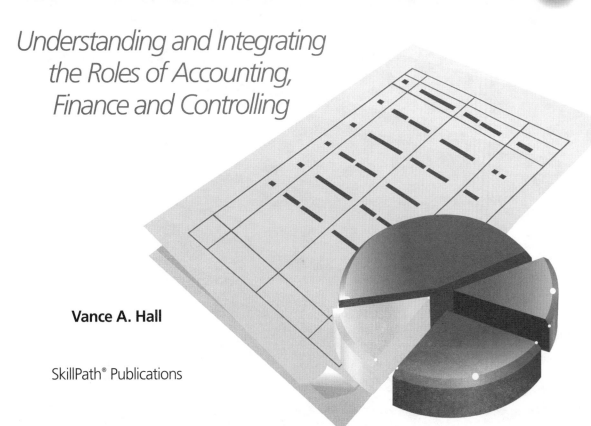

Vance A. Hall

SkillPath® Publications

Editor: Bill Cowles

Cover design and layout: Danielle Horn

ISBN: 978-1-934589-33-5

Printed in the United States of America

Table of Contents

Introduction

Welcome to the world of decision making. Decision making is the process of applying your knowledge of the past in the present, in an effort to second guess the future. Accounting, finance and controlling represent these three aspects of time: The Past, the Present and the Future. You learn from the past, you act in the present and you control (manage) the future. This book defines these three business areas and illustrates their relationships to each other in the management process. Illustration A shows the relationship on a time line and lists the related functions and activities.

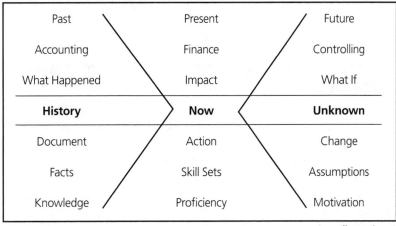

Past	Present	Future
Accounting	Finance	Controlling
What Happened	Impact	What If
History	**Now**	**Unknown**
Document	Action	Change
Facts	Skill Sets	Assumptions
Knowledge	Proficiency	Motivation

Illustration A

This book will help you understand what the accounting, financial analysis and controlling functions really are and will provide you with the tools to be an effective manager.

Part I – Accounting: The Recording of the Past

Part I provides an understanding of accounting and a working process for referencing accounting information from a non-financial manager's perspective. The hardest thing to understand about accounting is that it only tells us what has happened. It does not tell us what is happening or will happen. You cannot change or control the past; you can only document and learn from it. Therefore, the information you gain from the past is only as good as your documentation. In any system, if it's garbage in, it's garbage out. Managers must understand accounting so they can ensure the best information in to receive the best information out.

Part II – Finance: Understanding Accounting Information in the Present

Part II provides an understanding of finance and a working process for referencing the world of financial analysis and for the use of financial information from a non-financial manager's perspective. The hardest thing to understand about finance is that you can have the best financial analysis available, but it's worthless unless you can apply it in the present. You cannot plan or control the present; you can only act with the skill sets developed in the past. Therefore, you must continue to review all information so that it becomes real knowledge. *Webster's* defines knowledge as "Something learned and kept in mind." Managers must understand finance because financial analysis is the process for reviewing their past information.

Part III – Controlling: Using Accounting Information to Manage the Future

Part III provides an understanding of the Controller's function as an aid to management and an understanding of and reference for effectively using accounting and financial information in the management decision-making process. The hardest thing to understand about controlling is that it is an illusion; the future is an unknown. No one knows what tomorrow will be. You cannot really control the future; you can only have good forecasting, budgeting and controlling processes in place to manage your organization successfully. Therefore, you must understand and properly use controlling procedures, which are the manager's guide for successful decision making. The manager must also understand the functions of the Controller to be effective.

The mission of this book is to help non-financial managers understand that they can only record and learn from the past, act with information in the present, while planning for and controlling the future.

> **Note:** Managers must, therefore, understand accounting, financial analysis and controlling because it is the understanding of them that is "The Manager's Guide."

In the 21st century, if a business activity has a deliverable and a due date, it is classified as a project. In project management the most important steps are the defining of what is a part of the project, what is not, and a clear understanding of terminology.

This book is not intended to make you accountants or financial analysts. They represent highly trained professional careers. To properly master those positions takes an advanced college education. This book will, however, provide you a working understanding of the accounting and financial analysis functions, with key terminology that will aid you in your decision-making process.

This book is a unique and original look at accounting, finance and controlling from the non-financial manager's perspective. This book is not intended to be just another restating of previously published books, filled with references and no new information. Any references to previously published material, if appropriate, would be to college textbooks that are out of print, even if the information is timeless. Current textbooks will contain all the timeless materials and will be up to date on new principles, procedures and processes.

This book is not intended to put down accounting. Accounting is one of the most critical functions of a business. It is the misuse of accounting information that causes problems. The intent of this book is to provide non-financial managers with what they need to understand accounting and finance, which will allow them to properly use the information in their decision-making process.

> *Note:* In this book all Key Terms are capitalized and the **bolded** key terms are defined in the Key Terms section of Chapter 7 of each Part.

In the wonderful world of decision making, all business activities are a function of Economics. Economics is the principle of Supply and Demand, whether it is a business selling a product or service to a customer, a secretary typing a letter for the boss or an IT project manager installing a new computer system. What must be done is called demand; how it is to be done is called supply. And oh by the way, "You want it when?" This process is timeless; it is therefore recommended that your additional reading include a good college textbook on an introduction to economics for non-economic majors. It is surprising how very little has changed in the supply and demand process, even if modern technology has vastly changed how we process the information. The bottom line is still that *every decision is a guess*.

The 21st century function of supply and demand is called project management, which is still:

- The What, called Scope/Demand/Performance
- The How, called Resources/Supply
- The When, called Time/Change/Risk

These three are and always have been the three constraints of management. The college degree that demonstrates a comprehensive understanding of them is called an MBA (Master of Business Administration).

In conclusion, this book cannot provide you with an MBA or make you an accountant. It will, however, provide you with a functional working understanding of accounting (the past), finance (the present), controlling (the future), the What (called Scope/Demand/Performance), the How (called Resources/Supply), the When (called Time/Change/Risk), forecasting (the projecting of the What/Scope/Demand) and budgeting (the projecting of the How/Resources/Supply) that will aid you, the non-financial manager, in controlling (the phasing of the plan to reality) your organization through effective decision making (educated guessing about the future).

Part I
Accounting

Chapter 1:
History

Accounting is simply a process for tracking things of value, claims, income, expenses and cash. It has been around as long as man has had possessions. Even before man learned to write, he would count his sheep each morning to see if any had been taken by wolves. In modern times, this is called inventory control. Over the years, the accounting process has become more complex as our ability to record information has become more sophisticated. The bottom line is still, however: Do you have more today than you did yesterday?

The average worker looks at cash earned for their efforts versus cash spent for survival. A professional adds investment of excess cash earned—cash to be spent for future consumption. Businesses add long-term capital investment in buildings and other assets, along with trade credit for financing their expenses and their customer's purchases.

In modern times the confusion comes from the fact that businesses do not measure value in dollars, even though they report it in dollars. The easiest way to clarify this confusion is to explain the difference between cash accounting and accrual accounting. To do this, the following terms must be defined.

Revenue – Dollars earned for benefits provided. This is where the modern day confusion starts. It is dollars earned, not received. In the United States, modern day accounting tracks benefits, not dollars, when defining revenue. This varies in each country depending on Tax Codes. In the United States, taxes for businesses are based on when you earned the money by providing the benefits to the customer. It may have been a cash sale; however, quite often it is a credit sale and you will not receive the cash until some time in the future, maybe next year. These credit sales are called Accounts Receivable. The business must pay taxes now because it was earned, even though it has not been received yet. (For tax purposes, *individuals* only have to pay taxes on cash earned *and* received, so individuals can defer taxes by waiting until next year to be paid, even if they earned it this year.)

While this is true for yearly taxes, a closer look shows that the modern day employee, in the short-term, is not paid on a cash basis. Very few employees are day laborers who get paid cash at the end of each day's work. Most workers provide benefits today, but get paid in the future by what can be called salary or revenue. You work today, providing benefits to your employer, for which you will be paid in the future; thus, you have Accounts Receivable. Even if you quit tomorrow, your company owes you the money for today.

Expenses – Dollars owed for benefits consumed, whether you have paid for them or not. Here again, modern day accounting for businesses tracks benefits, not dollars. Therefore, a business may consume resources in December and claim it as an expense, even if they do not pay for it until next year. On the other hand, they may pay for it in December, but if they do not consume it, it is not an expense and the value must be carried over until next year as inventory. The dollars are accounted for, but not as a part of the Income Statement.

To demonstrate, imagine that the employee represents a small business and that they stop at a gas station on the way to work on Monday morning, put $40 dollars worth of gas into their car and put it on their credit card. Going to and from work during the week, they consume $15 worth of the gas. For accounting purposes, their gas expense is $15 (benefits consumed) even though they have not paid for it yet. The remaining $25 is carried over into the next period as inventory. If, on the other hand, the worker had paid cash for the gas, they as a business could still only claim a $15 gas expense (benefits consumed).

Profits – The net exchange of benefits (not dollars). The Income Statement combines Revenues (benefits provided) and Expenses (benefits consumed); the net is called Profits. A negative result is called Loss. Thus there are profits when the net is benefits provided and a loss when the net is benefits consumed. In business, profits are also referred to as Net Income or Net Earning. The confusion with modern day accounting is that these profits or losses are not actual dollars, even though they are presented in dollars.

Accrual Accounting vs. Cash Accounting – Accrual Accounting tracks benefits while Cash Accounting tracks dollars. As stated, the benefits in Accrual Accounting are measured and reported in dollars, but they are not real dollars paid or received. Many times a business owner will become confused, saying, "If I have all this revenue and profits, why don't I have any cash?" The accountant's answer is that the profits are in the form of accounts receivable, which must be collected, just like the employee has to wait until payday.

> **Note:** In modern times businesses do not measure value in dollars; Revenues and Expenses are measured in benefits.

Things will become clearer as you work your way through the following chapters, which will explain:

1. The **Accounting Equation** – the formula for keeping everything in balance

2. The **Accounting Cycle** – The process of recording and reporting financial information

3. The **Balance Sheet** – A statement of future benefits called Assets and the claims on those future benefits, called Liabilities and Equity

4. The **Income Statement** – A statement which reports benefits provided called Revenue, benefits consumed called Expenses and net difference called Profit and Loss or P&L

5. The **Cash Flow Statement** – A statement which reports actual dollars in and out

> **Note:** An important key to understanding accounting is that the Accounting Equation and Accounting Cycle are used to produce the financial statements, and that the Balance Sheet looks at future benefits vs. claims, the Income Statement tracks past benefits and the Cash Flow Statement tracks dollars.

In summary, each of the chapters will define additional accounting and financial terms, which will provide you, the non-financial manager, with an understanding of the accounting process.

Key Point Review (answers on page 163)

1. Revenue is dollars earned/received for _____.

2. Expenses are dollars owed/paid for _____.

3. Profits are the _____.

4. Accrual Accounting tracks _____.

5. Cash Accounting tracks _____.

6. The bottom line in accounting is: Do you have _____ ?

7. Accounting is a process for tracking _____.

8. Profits do not measure value in _____.

9. Profits measure value in _____.

10. The purpose of accounting is to track the past and generate the _____.

Chapter 2:
Accounting Equation

The Accounting Equation is a function of double-entry accounting. When people add a column of numbers more than once, they often end up with different answers. In the 1500s, an Italian monk developed double-entry accounting in order to eliminate these arithmetic errors. You take two sets of the same numbers (Illustration I-2-1), put them in different orders and add them. If the totals are equal they must be correct. Double-entry accounting uses this principle with two simple rules. First, the equation must always be equal (called in balance); the things of value must always equal the claims. Second, the total value of all left-hand entries must equal the total value of all right-hand entries.

"It doesn't equal 5000" model

Cover the first column with a piece of paper, then slide it down, adding the numbers out loud quickly. You would be surprised at how many people come up with 5000. This is hard to demonstrate in a book, but in a group everyone comes up with 5000 the first time. Double-entry accounting eliminates these mathematical errors by adding the numbers twice in different orders, called taking a **Trial Balance**. If the two results are the same, there can be no errors.

$1000	10
40	1000
1000	20
30	1000
1000	30
20	1000
1000	40
$ 10	$ 1000

Illustration I-2-1

To understand this process, the following terms must be defined:

- **Assets** – The things of value (future benefits) measured in monetary terms at cost that are owned or controlled by the organization

- **Liabilities/debt** – The claims of the creditors

- **Equity** – The claims of the owners

Note: These three parts of the Accounting Equation—Assets, Liabilities and Owner's Equity—make up the Balance Sheet.

These are the three principal parts of the Accounting Equation and the first rule, that the thing of value must equal the claims.

The formula is stated:

$$\text{Assets} = \text{Liabilities} + \text{Owner's Equity}$$

In this format, the equation represents the Balance Sheet. (The Balance Sheet will be discussed in detail in Chapter 4.) In practice, some confusion develops because different names are used for these three parts of the accounting equation, depending on the size and type of business. A closer look at the definitions will help to clarify this.

Assets are almost always called assets. They represent the future benefits of the organization or resources that can be deployed at some time after the date of the Balance Sheet. In modern day accounting, the value of these assets must be recorded at cost. It is very important at this time to understand the difference between Cost and Expense; they are not the same.

> *Cost* is dollars owed/spent for future benefits. *Expenses* (as defined in Chapter 1) are dollars owed/spent for benefits consumed. Using the example of purchasing $40 worth of gas, you have at the time of purchase a future benefit (asset) of $40 worth of gas. As you drive to and from work during the week, you consume $15 worth of the gas. So at the end of week one, you have a remaining asset of $25 worth of gas, which can be consumed in the future, and an expense of $15 for the gas consumed, which will be reported on the Income Statement (see Chapter 5). You could, of course, say that the gas consumed cost $15. *Don't.*

Liabilities, which are the claims of the creditors, are often called debt; however, on Balance Sheets they are nearly always called liabilities. Sometimes liabilities are referred to as creditor's equity, which it is. In practice, however, this is not done because it becomes confused with owner's equity. *The thing to remember is that **equity** simply means claim.* Therefore, creditor's equity is the creditor's claims on the Assets and owner's equity is the owner's claims. When you hear terms like liabilities or debt, you can say, "Ah, the creditor's claims."

Owner's Equity has many names, based on the size and type of business. They include: Net Worth, Equity, Owner's Equity, Organizational Equity (for non-profits), Stockholder's Equity, which is Capital Stock, and Retained Earnings (see Chapter 4). If you see the term Equity by itself, it is supposed to mean Owner's Equity. The term **Equities**, however, means claims and could include liabilities.

The Accounting Equation is, therefore:

$$\text{Assets (future benefits at cost)} = \text{Liabilities (creditor's claims)} + \text{Owner's Equity (owner's claims)}$$

Modern day accounting requires the equation to be expanded to itemize the Income Statement. To properly report income you need to separate it from the existing equation. Since the Income Statement reports Profits and Loss, you look at the Accounting Equation to see which of the three parts is affected by profit and loss; it is Owner's Equity. The owner has a claim on the profits and is responsible for the losses. The two functions that generate profit/loss are Revenue and Expenses. Revenue increases Owner's Equity and Expenses reduce it.

The Accounting Equation is restated as:

Assets (future benefits at cost) = Liabilities (creditor's claims) + Owner's Equity (owner's claims) + Revenue (dollars earned/received for benefits provided) – Expenses (dollars owed/spent for benefits consumed); or

$$\text{Assets} = \text{Liabilities} + \text{Owner's Equity} + \text{Revenue} - \text{Expenses}$$

> **Note:** These two new parts of the Accounting Equation, Revenue and Expenses, make up the Income Statement.

To understand how accountants use this equation, one point must be clarified. In accounting, all account balances are normally positive numbers. For Assets, Liabilities, Owner's Equity and Revenue, it is clear because there are plus signs in front of them. People, however, have trouble seeing expenses as a positive number because of the minus sign. Think about it. If you owe the gas station $40, it is a real $40. Likewise, the $15 worth of gas consumed is a real $15. The minus sign in the equation subtracts it. For training purposes, a little algebra is applied and expenses are moved to the left side by adding plus expenses to both sides.

$$\text{Assets} + \text{Expenses} = \text{Liabilities} + \text{Owner's Equity} + \text{Revenue} - \text{Expenses} + \text{Expenses}$$

The expenses on the right side cancel each other out.

$$\text{Assets} + \text{Expenses} = \text{Liabilities} + \text{Owner's Equity} + \text{Revenue}$$

This makes it easier to understand double-entry accounting, which uses **Accounts** to record transactions. Each account has a positive and a negative side and can be represented by a **T Account** (see Illustration I-2-2). For Assets and Expenses, which are on the left-hand side of the equal sign when positive, the positive side is on the left of the T account and the negative is on the right. For Liabilities, Owner's Equity and Revenue, which are on the right-hand side of the equal sign when positive, the positive side is on the right of the T account and the negative is on the left. Therefore, the increases to Assets and Expenses are always on the left side, as shown by the up arrows, and decreases are on the right side, shown by the down arrows. The opposite is true for Liabilities, Owner's Equity and Revenue, which are increased on the right side, shown by the up arrows, and decreased on the left side, shown by the down arrows.

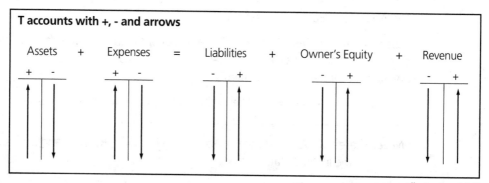

Illustration I-2-2

A problem with terminology developed, which required the creation of two new terms. It would sound funny or confusing if, after making a left-hand entry to an asset account, you said you lefted the account, or after a right-hand entry, that you righted the account. People might ask, "What do you mean you righted the account? What was wrong with it?" To clarify this problem, two new words were created: **Debit** and **Credit**. These words have confused people for centuries; however, they need never confuse you again. *Debit* simply means "left." *Credit* simply means "right." These terms have taken on additional meanings, like credit card or debit card, but in the accounting process, debit is a left-hand entry (see Illustration I-2-3). For Assets and Expenses, debits are pluses and credits are negatives; and for Liabilities, Owner's Equity and Revenue, credits are pluses and debits are negatives.

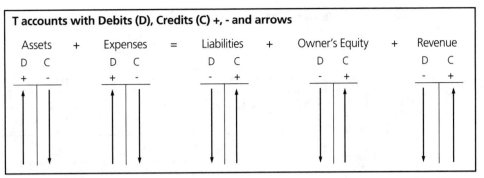

T accounts with Debits (D), Credits (C) +, - and arrows

Assets	+	Expenses	=	Liabilities	+	Owner's Equity	+	Revenue
D C		D C		D C		D C		D C
+ -		+ -		- +		- +		- +

Illustration I-2-3

When you add to cash (an asset) you debit the cash account, and when you spend cash you credit the account. When you add to debt (liabilities) you credit the account and when you pay off debt you debit it. Debit cards get their name because when you use one to get cash out of your checking account, you reduce the bank's debt to you. The bank debits your account, which is a liability for the bank.

Chapter 3: Accounting Cycle will demonstrate how the accounting equation is used to maintain accurate accounts.

In summary, the Accounting Equation uses the double-entry process to eliminate arithmetic errors and facilitate Accrual Accounting.

Key Point Review (answers on page 163)

1. The five parts of the Accounting Equation are: _____, _____, _____ , _____ and_____.

2. Define Assets:_____

3. Define Cost: _____

4. Define Liabilities:_____

5. Define Owner's Equity: _____

6. The two rules of accounting are _____
   and_____.

7. Even though Owner's Equity is often referred to as just Equity, the term "equities" means _____.

8. The Accounting Equation uses something called _____.

9. _____ accounts are used to represent the positive and negative side of entries.

10. For accounting purposes, left is called _____ and right is called _____.

Chapter 3:
Accounting Cycle

The Accounting Cycle applies the Accounting Equation in a six-step process (see Illustration I-3-1).

Accounting Cycle					
Step 1	Step 2	Step 3	Step 4	Step 5	Step 6
Classify accounting transactions	Record to General Journal	Post to General Ledger	Adjust entries 6 types	Close permanent & temporary accounts	Generate financial reports

Once the reports have been generated, the accounting department repeats the cycle for the next period.

Illustration I-3-1

Step 1 is to classify accounting transactions. A person may ask, "Isn't it everything we do in business?" The answer is no; in fact, very few daily activities are accounting transactions.

Accounting Transactions are business activities that can readily be identified in monetary terms. Examples include buying supplies and getting a receipt, selling a product or service, paying a bill, receiving a payment from a customer or borrowing money. In some companies, like a law office, professionals and staff may be on billable minutes so that their time can be accounted for in monetary terms. Most daily activities are, however, not readily identifiable in monetary terms. Examples include talking on the phone for ten minutes, spending twenty minutes preparing a report, working for half an hour with an employee. These activities are covered in the big picture when you are paid your salary, but each individual event is not an accounting transaction because it cannot readily be assigned a dollar value.

Note: Actual Accounting Transactions represent only a small portion of business activities.

T accounts

(10) Cash		(11) Accounts Receivable		(12) Supplies/Inventory	
Debit	Credit	Debit	Credit	Debit	Credit

(13) Wagon		(20) Supplies Expense		(30) Accounts Payable	
Debit	Credit	Debit	Credit	Debit	Credit

(31) Bank Notes Payable		(40) Sidewalk Swigs Capital		(50) Sales Revenue	
Debit	Credit	Debit	Credit	Debit	Credit

Illustration I-3-2

Once an accounting transaction has been identified it is classified using the T accounts (see Illustration I-3-2). T accounts are grouped within the five parts of the accounting equation and listed in the **Chart of Accounts** (see Illustration I-3-3), which is the table of contents for the General Ledger. The General Ledger will be discussed in Step 3.

Chart of Accounts (The Table of Contents for the General Ledger)

Chart of Accounts	Chart of Accounts
For this training exercise:	As used by your company:
Assets (10s, 100s, 1000s, etc.)	Assets (10s, 100s, 1000s, etc.)
(10) Cash	
(11) Accounts Receivable	equals
(12) Supplies/Inventory	
(13) Wagon	
Expenses (20s, 200s, 2000s, etc.)	Liabilities (20s, 200s, 2000s, etc.)
(20) Supplies Expense	plus
Liabilities (30s, 300s, 3000s, etc.)	Owner's Equity (30s, 300s, 3000s, etc.)
(30) Accounts Payable	
(31) Bank Notes Payable	plus
Owners Equity (40s, 400s, 4000s, etc.)	Revenue (40s, 400s, 4000s, etc.)
(40) Sidewalk Swigs, Capital	minus
Revenue (50s, 500s, 5000s, etc.)	Expenses (5xxxs, 6xxxs, 7xxxs)
(50) Sales Revenue	

Illustration I-3-3

The transaction is first classified as an Asset (future benefits at cost), a Liability (creditor's claims), Owner's Equity (owner's claims), Revenue (dollars earned/received for benefits provided) or an Expense (dollars owed/spent for benefits consumed). It is then assigned to the appropriate account within the proper group, using double-entry accounting. Once the current group of transactions has been classified and entered into the T accounts (see Illustrations I-3-4a, I-3-4b and I-3-4c), a **Trial Balance** is taken by adding all the debit entries and all the credit entries, respectively. If the two balances are equal, there should be no arithmetic errors.

Statement of Transactions

1. We start the business with $100 by opening a checking account under the name of Sidewalk Swigs, Inc.

2. We decide to offer home delivery and purchase a wagon for $25. We make a down payment of $5 and borrow the rest from our friendly banker.

3. We open an account at our friendly local grocery store for supplies and purchase $50 in fruit punch supplies on credit.

4. We cater a birthday party on our block, billing the Smith family $40.

5. The Smith family sends us a check for $10; the remainder will be paid next month.

6. We pay $10 on our account at our friendly local grocery store.

7. We take our end-of-month inventory of supplies to determine how much was used up. We note that $35 of our original $50 inventory is left.

Illustration I-3-4a

T accounts

(10) Cash			(11) Accounts Receivable			(12) Supplies/Inventory		
Debit		Credit	Debit		Credit	Debit		Credit
(1) 100		5 (2)	(4) 40		10 (5)	(3) 50		15 (7)
(5) 10		10 (6)						

(13) Wagon			(20) Supplies Expense			(30) Accounts Payable		
Debit		Credit	Debit		Credit	Debit		Credit
(2) 25			(7) 15			(6) 10		50 (3)

(31) Bank Notes Payable			(40) Sidewalk Swigs Capital			(50) Sales Revenue		
Debit		Credit	Debit		Credit	Debit		Credit
		20 (2)			100 (1)			40 (4)

Illustration I-3-4b

Trial Balance:

(Total all Debits and Credits respectively)

Debits	Credits
$100	$ 5
10	10
40	10
50	15
25	50
15	20
10	100
	40
$250	$250

Illustration I-3-4c

Step 2 is to record these transactions in the **General Journal**. The General Journal is also called the book of original entry (see Illustration I-3-5). The General Journal has five columns, as shown. All transactions are to be recorded in chronological order. Once recorded, any changes must be carefully documented. Any changes made to the General Journal that have not been documented, if material in value, may be considered by the government as an attempt to defraud. The General Journal is one of the most important documents and must be safeguarded. If you lose all your financial records, they can be recreated from the General Journal. Any good college accounting textbook can explain this process and the laws in greater detail.

Journal Entries

Date/#	Item	Ref.	Debit	Credit
1	Cash	10	$100	
	Sidewalk Swigs, Capital			$100
	Start business			
2	Wagon		5	
	Cash		20	
	Bank Loan, Payable			25
	2 years @ 8%			
3	Supplies/Inventory		50	
	Accounts Payable			50
	2/10 net 30			

Illustration I-3-5

Step 3 is posting (copying) the transaction parts into the individual accounts in the **General Ledger**. One by one, each line item in the General Journal is posted to the proper General Ledger account (see Illustration I-3-6). The General Ledger keeps track of the balances in each account. These accounts have seven columns, of which the last two are used to maintain a running balance. This balance for Assets and Expenses, which are on the left side of the Accounting Equation when positive, are normally debits and, respectively, the normal balances for Liabilities, Owner's Equity and Revenue are credits.

Ledger Entries

General Ledger

#10	Cash					
Date/#	Item	Ref	Debit	Credit	Debit	Credit
1			$100		$100	
2				5	95	
5			10		105	
6				10	95	

Illustration I-3-6

These first three steps are repeated for as long as the business is in operation. Each monetary transaction is classified, recorded and posted. For owners and managers to use this information, it is summarized periodically into reports—monthly, quarterly or annually. However, the reports can be generated using Steps 4, 5 and 6 at any time.

At the end of a reporting period—for example, the end of the year—the books are adjusted and closed and the financial statements are generated: The Balance Sheet (see Chapter 4), the Income Statement (see Chapter 5) and the Cash Flow Statement (see Chapter 6).

Step 4 involves the **Adjusting Entries**. There are six types of adjusting entries (see Illustration I-3-7). (For a detailed understanding of them, refer to a good college accounting textbook.) These accounting entries are made by the accounting department at the point in time when the books are closed.

Adjusting Entries

Deferrals	Accruals
1. Inventory/supplies	5. Unbilled Earned Revenue
2. Depreciation of Capital Assets	6. Accrued Expenses like wages
3. Prepaid Expenses	
4. Unearned Revenue	

1. Beginning Inventory + Purchases − Ending Inventory = Inventory Expenses
      $40,000   + $20,000 − $35,000   = $25,000

2. Purchase Price / Useful Life = Depreciation Expenses
      $315,000   / 31.25 years= $10,000

Note: For assets like equipment and vehicles, a salvage value, which is the anticipated value of the asset at the end of its useful life, must be calculated and subtracted from the purchase price.

Illustration I-3-7

Two of the six types will be used to demonstrate the adjusting process.

The first is adjusting entries for inventory and supplies. **Inventory** is normally assets which are or become a part of the finished product delivered to the customer. **Supplies** are normally assets consumed in the day-to-day operations of a business, like paper and pens. The adjusting process is the same for both inventory and supplies (see Illustration I-3-7). The process starts with the beginning value, which for a new business may be zero. Then all purchases are added. Finally, a physical inventory is taken and subtracted. The sum represents the value of what has gone out the door (hopefully the front door) in inventory delivered or supplies consumed. It also includes waste materials and shrinkage (theft).

The second adjusting entry is for **Depreciation** (see Illustration I-3-7) which accounts for the use of buildings, vehicles and equipment, called **Capital Assets**. This adjusting process starts with the purchase price, called **Cost Basis**. This represents the actual dollar amount paid/owed for the asset. Then the useful life is determined using the Internal Revenue Service's Tax Codes. For example assume a useful life of 31½ years for a new building. Therefore, if you paid $315,000 for the building, you could claim $10,000 depreciation expense each year. The tax codes are continually changing so, for your useful life, be sure to consult current tax codes.

All these adjusting entries must be made to ensure that you are reporting fairly your financial condition on your financial statements.

Step 5 closes the accounts for the period. There are two types of accounts: Permanent and Temporary. Revisiting Chapter 2 about the Accounting Equation, the three original parts consisted of Assets, Liabilities and Equity. All the accounts in these three parts are **Permanent Accounts** because they carry forward into future periods. These accounts are not really closed; they are balanced to show the values that will be reported on the Balance Sheet and carried forward. The two remaining parts of the Accounting Equation which were added, Revenue and Expenses, are **Temporary Accounts** used to show what happened during the reported period. These accounts must be closed and summarized as Profits or Losses into Owner's Equity. Each period, these accounts must be reset to zero (see Illustration I-3-8a). The closed accounts will form the Income Statement and the balanced accounts will form the Balance Sheet (see Illustration I-3-8b).

Closed and balanced T accounts

(10) Cash			(11) Accounts receivable			(12) Supplies inventory	
(1) 100	5 (2)		(4) 40	10 (5)		(3) 50	15 (7)
(5) 10	10 (6)			30(B2)			35(B3)
	95(B1)						
(B1) 95			(B2) 30			(B3) 35	

(13) Wagon			(20) Supplies expense			(30) Accounts Payable	
(2) 25	25(B4)		(7) 15	15(C1)		(6) 10	50 (3)
						(B5) 40	
(B4) 25							40(B5)

(31) Bank notes payable			(40) Sidewalk Swigs, Capital			(50) Sales revenue	
(B6) 20	20 (2)			100 (1)		(C2) 40	40 (4)
			(B7)125	25			
			(C3)				
	20(B6)			125(B7)		(B1) 95	

Income Summary	
(C1) 15	40(C2)
(C3) 25	

Illustration I-3-8a

Financial Statements

Sidewalk Swigs, Inc.

Income Statement—June 20XX

Sales revenue $40

Expenses:

    Supplies expense 15

Net income $25

Sidewalk Swigs, Inc.

Balance Sheet—June 30, 20XX

Assets		Equities	
Cash $95		Accounts payable $40	
Accounts receivable 30		Bank notes payable 20	
Supplies inventory 35		Total current liabilities $60	
Total current assets $160		Owner's Equity	
Wagon 25		Sidewalk Swigs, Capital 125	
Total Assets $185		Total Liabilities and Equity $185	

Illustration I-3-8b

Step 6 in the Accounting Cycle is generating the Balance Sheet, the Income Statement and the Cash Flow Statement.

> **Note:** Accounting is required by law to be done correctly and in a timely manner. This may explain why the accounting department must be so rigid in its process demands.

In summary, this process is repeated each period. It must be done in a timely manner. If invoices or expense reports are not turned in when required so that the transactions can be properly reported within the proper period, the financial statements are *false*. If the amounts involved are material, it becomes a federal offense. If false financial statements are being used in regard to bank loans, the organization is committing bank fraud, which is a jailable offense. *This is serious!*

Key Point Review (answers on page 163)

1. The Accounting Cycle has _____ steps.

2. Accounting transactions which are classified with T accounts are _____.

3. Are all business activities accounting transactions? _____

4. Transactions are recorded in the _____.

5. Transactions are posted to the _____.

6. Adjusting entries are made by the _____.

7. Permanent accounts are _____ , _____ and _____.

8. Temporary accounts are_____ and _____.

9. The Accounting Cycle generates the _____, _____
   and_____.

10. Failure to properly report all expenses on a timely basis, if material, becomes
    a_____.

Chapter 4:
Balance Sheet

The Balance Sheet reports two things: **Future Benefits** and **Claims**. **Assets** are future benefits at cost. **Claims** are **Liabilities** (the claims of creditors) and **Equity** (the claims of owners).

The **Balance Sheet** reports the financial health of an organization at a given instant in time, which is midnight on the date of the Balance Sheet. Using a normal calendar year for the business's accounting year, called the **Fiscal Year**, the books are closed and the financial statements are produced for December 31, 20XX. By noon on January 1, however, many of the financial values may have changed; cash may have been received or payments made.

The best way to understand the Balance Sheet is to think about it as an x-ray or snapshot. Your doctor takes your x-ray. As you are leaving the hospital you get hit by a truck. Your next x-ray will be different. The same is true of the Balance Sheet. A current Balance Sheet is one for the close of business yesterday, with footnotes about anything that has happened so far today.

It would not be reasonable to be creating the financial statements every day. It is important to understand, however, that just like the x-ray, the further you get away from the date of the Balance Sheet, the greater the number of changes. The Balance Sheet is only a reference to a point in time and must be used properly.

The two sections of the Balance Sheet are divided into five parts for effective analysis of the information (see Illustration I-4-1).

Balance Sheet five parts

Balance Sheet

Assets
    Current Assets
    Fixed Assets

Liabilities & Equity
    Current Liabilities
    Long-term Debt
    Owner's Equity

Illustration I-4-1

The **Assets** are the future benefits, like cash which can be spent, receivables which can be collected, inventory which can be sold and equipment which can be used. These Assets are divided into two parts: Current Assets and Fixed (Non-current) Assets.

Balance Sheet

MOHAWK LAWN SERVICE CO.
Balance Sheet as of December 31, 20XX

Assets

Current
Cash		$975	
Receivables (after subtracting $5 for estimated amount uncollectible)		20	
Inventories, supplies		100	
Prepayments		50	$1,145

Non-current
Shed	$75		
Equipment	225		
	$300		
Less: Amount charged off as depreciation	60	240	240
			$1,385

Equities

Current Liabilities
Taxes payable	$125	
Wages payable	400	
Interest payable	30	
Dividends payable	25	$580

Long-term Debt
Loan payable, 10% due in 20XX		300
		880

Stockholder's equity
Capital stock, par $1	$100	
Retained earnings	405	505
		$1,385

Illustration I-4-2

Current Assets – Those Assets that will be used up or turned over *within one year*

Fixed Assets – All Non-current Assets. Take a minute to reflect on this. Current Assets are carefully defined; all other Assets are Fixed Assets.

Claims are divided into three parts:

1. *Current Liabilities* – All claims of creditors that are due and payable *within one year*

> **Note:** The one year for Current Assets and Current Liabilities is critical and will be explained in Part II, Chapter 2, Ratio Analysis.

2. *Long-term Debt* – All non-current claims of the creditors

3. *Owner's Equity* – The claims of the owners. For non-profit organizations this may be called organizational worth, equity or net worth, since the organization owns itself.

Owner's Equity is in theory what is left after the creditors have taken their share of the assets. A problem arises, however, in that the values of the assets are required to be at cost, not market. If a building which cost $315,000 has been depreciated for 10 years at $10,000 a year, the new Balance Sheet value (called Book Value or new **Cost Basis**) would be $315,000 minus $100,000 which equals $215,000. The real value, however, because of inflation, may be much more, maybe $400,000. Accrual Accounting does not recognize the $400,000 until the building is sold. Therefore, the Owner's Equity does not show the additional Market Value. The opposite could also be true where, because of poor maintenance, the building is rundown and only worth $150,000. Owner's Equity would now have $65,000 of value ($215,000 – $150,000) that does not exist.

To adjust for this and make complete disclosure, these differences are footnoted. In fact, footnotes are required whenever the information is not obvious and material. In the case of the building, there must be a footnote citing a **Fee Appraisal** estimate of the Market Value.

For a detailed explanation of the Balance Sheet, refer to a good college accounting textbook. A general overview of the Balance Sheet is as follows (refer back to Illustration I-4-2):

Current Assets are very limited, comprising the following:

- *Cash* – Real cash in hand or in bank accounts

- *Marketable Securities* – A holding place for cash that provides higher interest, but carries risks

- *Accounts Receivable* – The money owed to the company from its customer's purchases that it financed. This entry must always include a set-aside for uncollectibles.

Inventory – Currently, all inventory must be reported at cost. Some exceptions may exist for very old companies.

Prepaid Items – These are items like insurance.

The preceding list, which is often complex in nature, makes up the Current Assets. All other assets are fixed, including **cash** if it's part of a **Sinking Fund** (savings account) that is not going to be spent within the next *one year*.

Fixed Assets are divided into two parts:

> ***Note:*** Fixed Assets may be called many different things such as Non-current or Plant. Just remember that Current Assets are those assets that will be used up or turned over within one year; everything else is a Fixed Asset.

1. *Tangible Fixed Assets* – The real assets like buildings, vehicles, equipment and cash in long-term sinking funds

2. *Intangible Fixed Assets* – The paper assets like copyrights, patents, goodwill or oil reserves. The accounting process for the use of Tangible Fixed Assets is called depreciation, for the Intangible Fixed Assets it is called amortization. The process is the same for both even if the names are different. The different names help to clarify the assets to which the process is applied.

Liabilities are the creditor's claims and are divided into two parts:

1. *Current Liabilities* – Short-term debt due and payable within one year. This debt is normally identified as accrued or payable—Accrued Salaries, Accrued Taxes or Accounts Payable, Taxes Payable, Dividends Payable. Current Liabilities also include the current (due within one year) portion of Long-term Debt.

2. *Long-term Debt* – All non-current liabilities like bonds

Owner's Equity, called **Stockholder's Equity** for corporations, is divided into two sections:

1. *Capital Stock* – The monetary value actually invested in the company by the owners through the purchase of stock

2. *Retained Earnings* – The profits from prior periods not paid out in dividends, but retained and reinvested in the company on behalf of the owners. Retained Earnings will be a negative number if there are too many losses.

In summary, the Balance Sheet is a cross-sectional look at the financial health of the business at midnight on the date of the Balance Sheet. It compares the future benefits at cost (Assets) with the claims (Liabilities and Equity) against them. Remember, material real value differences must be footnoted.

Key Point Review (answers on page 163)

1. The Balance Sheet reports two things:_____ and_____.

2. Assets are _____.

3. Claims are _____ and _____.

4. The Balance Sheet reports an instant in time similar to an_____.

5. The five parts of the Balance Sheet are _____ ,_____,
   _____ ,_____ and _____.

6. The definitions of Current Assets and Current Liabilities have _____
   in common.

7. If any of the financial statements have information that is unclear and material, it must
   be_____.

8. All Assets must be recorded at _____.

9. The future benefits (Assets) and the claims must always _____.

10. Retained Earnings are _____.

The Non-financial Manager's Guide to Business Decision Making

Chapter 5:
Income Statement

The **Income Statement** covers events during the period of time between Balance Sheets. For a new business, the beginning Balance Sheet is all zeros. The normal beginning Balance Sheet for a period is the Balance Sheet for the end of the last reporting period.

It is important to remember that the Income Statement reports benefits delivered (Revenue), benefits consumed (Expenses) and the net difference **(Profits/Loss)**. The Income Statement does not reflect anything about cash, which will be discussed in the next chapter.

> **Note:** It is true that some revenue is from cash sales and that companies generally report cash and credit sales separately, but not always. Also, many expenses are paid in cash, but you cannot tell which ones from the Income Statement.

The Income Statement matches the dollars earned/received from benefits delivered in a period with the dollars owed/spent for benefits consumed in the period which were necessary to provide the benefits delivered. This is called the **Matching Principle**, which forms the basis for Accrual Accounting. As a result, a properly prepared Income Statement shows the net increase or decrease from operations in the Net Worth of the company after the exchange of benefits. This, given certain adjustments like **Extraordinary Items** (expenses that are not a normal part of business operations), is taxable income. Some people then ask, "How can it be taxable if I have not been paid the cash?" The answer is the difference between Cash Accounting (personal income) and Accrual Accounting (business income). With personal income, it is not taxable until you receive the cash, so you can defer it for tax proposes by putting it in a 401(k). Business income is earned and taxable when the benefits are delivered to the customer, even if it takes you years to collect it. In general, the Internal Revenue Service, with some exceptions, does not want businesses deferring taxable income.

The Income Statement for publicly traded corporations normally has four parts (see Illustration I-5-1): Revenues, Expenses, Net Income with a statement of change in retained earnings, and a section that states several items, like earnings, on a per-share basis. For businesses that are not publicly traded, smaller businesses and non-profits, the per-share and change-to-retained earnings portions are most often omitted.

Income Statement

SIDEWALK SWIGS, INC.
Income Statement for the Year 20XX

Revenues
Sales (Less: Uncollectibles of $10)		$1,490
Other income		72
		$1,562

Revenue deductions
Expenses
Cost of goods sold	$800	
Selling	150	
Administrative	160	$1,110
Income taxes		45
Income before extraordinary item		407
Uninsured storm loss		75
Net income		332
Retained earnings at beginning of year		
As previously reported	$500	
Adjustments for litigation losses of prior years	135	
As restated		$365
		$697
Cash dividends on common stock, 25¢ per share		25
Retained earnings at end of year		$672

Per share of common stock
Income before extraordinary item	$3.99
Extraordinary item (storm loss)	[.74]
Net income	$3.25

Illustration I-5-1

Revenue – Dollars earned/received for benefits provided. The Revenue section for big businesses has several parts. First, all revenue from all sales, called **Total Revenue**, must be stated, even if a customer returns the item, negating the sale. Often, Total Revenue itemizes cash and credit sales. Second, all returns, allowances, rebates, discounts and certain sales that are uncollectible (those related to sales made during the period) are subtracted from Total Revenue to give **Net Revenue**, generally called **Net Sales**. Net Sales for financial analysis purposes is 100% of Sales. Other Income (Income from sources other than operations) is then added to Net Sales. Examples of Other Income are interest income or gain on the sale of an asset.

Expenses – The dollars owed/paid for benefits consumed. Expenses are normally divided into three parts: Cost of Goods Sold (COGS)/Cost of Sales, Operating Expenses and Extraordinary Items.

Cost of Goods Sold/Cost of Sales accounts for direct costs associated with the sale like the purchase of inventory, shipping or direct labor for a manufacturing company. Companies want to apply all the direct costs possible to the sale to provide the best cost accounting. Often, the price is a markup on this figure. In a service company, the cost of goods is not shown because the value is normally zero.

Operating Expenses – The general expenses of doing business. Operating Expenses are all necessary expenses that cannot be conveniently associated with each sale. They often include all the support activities which make up overhead. The total of these expenses is subtracted from Revenue; the difference is called Operating Income. Extraordinary Expenses (all expenses not associated with normal operations, like snow removal in Miami) are subtracted from Operating Income; the difference is called **Net Income** (sometimes referred to as **Net Earnings**).

Net Income – The net difference between benefits provided and benefits consumed, called Profit/Loss. The taxes and any declared dividends are then subtracted, leaving the change in retained earnings. Some Income Statements show the beginning retained earnings, add the gain or loss and show the ending retained earnings, which is stated on the Balance Sheet.

Earnings per Share – The Net Income divided by the number of outstanding shares. This last section shows selected items on a per-share basis. The most import is Earnings per Share. If the Net Income is $322 and there are 102 shares outstanding, then the Earnings per Share would be $3.25. This is done because stockholders want to know what their shares earned. Example: If the shareholder had 50 shares, their earnings for the period would be 50 times $3.25, which equals $162.50.

Note: Remember, the Income Statement reports the net exchange of benefits, not dollars.

In summary, the Income Statement reports the net increase (profits) or decrease (loss) of value to an organization from operations. The use of this information in understanding the business's operations will be discussed in Part II – Finance.

Key Point Review (answers on page 163)

1. The Income Statement covers the time between _____.

2. Relating the benefits consumed in a period with the benefits they helped to provide is called the_____.

3. Extraordinary items are expenses that are not a part of _____.

4. Total revenue less all returns, allowances, etc. is called_____.

5. Cost of Goods Sold expenses must be conveniently assigned to the _____.

6. Revenue is_____.

7. Expenses are _____.

8. Net income (profit/loss) is the _____.

9. Earnings Per Share is reported because _____.

10. The Income Statement reports the net increase or decrease in _____, not necessarily dollars.

Chapter 6:
Cash Flow Statement

The **Cash Flow Statement** reconciles actual cash in and out. This is critical because sales may be rapidly increasing, but since the sales may be on credit, there may not be any cash to pay the expenses incurred. One of the primary causes of failure of successful businesses is uncontrolled growth. The company just cannot support the cash flow.

> ***Note:*** Of all the financial reports, many manufacturing executives consider this the most important. For them, it reports the real bottom line by answering the question "Are you bleeding to death?"

Cash, often called **Circulating Capital**, is the lifeblood of the business. A healthy business, like a healthy athlete, can bleed to death in a very short time if an artery is cut. For the athlete, the loss of blood must be stopped and, likewise, the business must stop a cash drain.

The Cash Flow Statement cannot measure Profit/Loss, because they are the exchange of benefits as reported on the Income Statement. The Cash Flow Statement cannot measure the financial health of the business, because that is the relationship between future benefits and claims as reported on the Balance Sheet. The Cash Flow Statement and the Current Ratio (See Part II, Chapter 2) monitor the life blood or simply your ability to be effective in the short run. A shortage of cash, like a shortage of blood for an athlete, can cause a healthy entity to perform poorly.

The Cash Flow Statement has three parts: Cash flow from **Operations**, cash flow from **Investing** and cash flow from **Borrowing** (see Illustration I-6-1).

```
Cash Flow Statement
                    SIDEWALK SWIGS, INC.
              Cash Flow Statement for the Year 20XX

              Cash Flows From Operating Activities
Net income ..................................................................... $10
Accounts receivable increase ........................................... (10)
Inventory increase ............................................................ (25)
Prepayments increase ....................................................... (15)
Depreciation expense ........................................................ 15
Accounts payable increase ............................................... 20
Taxes payable increase .................................................... 5
Accrued expenses increase ............................................... 5        $20

              Cash Flows From Investing Activities
Purchases of property, plant and equipment ............................... ($25)

              Cash Flows From Financing Activities
Short-term borrowings ..................................................... 0
Long-term borrowings ..................................................... 10
Capital stock issue .......................................................... 200
Cash dividends to stockholders ......................................... 0        $210

Net increase in cash during year ............................................... $205
```

Illustration I-6-1

1. Cash Flow from **Operations** starts with the Net Profit/Loss. If the organization was on a cash basis, this would be cash flow. Corporations, however, must be on Accrual Accounting, so Net Profit/Loss includes non-cash sales in the form of benefits provided and benefits consumed where no cash has changed hands.

   In addition to Profits/Losses, there are three sets of transactions to be considered: the net change in Current Assets, the net change in Current Liabilities and Depreciation. The net change refers to the changes in Current Assets and Current Liabilities between the beginning Balance Sheet and the end of the period Balance Sheet. Remember, the Income Statement reports what happens between these two Balance Sheets.

Net changes in Current Assets. Example: If the beginning Inventory balance was $20,000 and the ending Inventory balance was $25,000, the change in Inventory would be plus $5,000. This means the organization has purchased an additional $5,000 worth of inventory and has spent $5,000 cash. For all the Current Asset accounts, if this change (called the delta, represented by a ▲ in mathematics) is positive, it means cash out, and if the change is negative, it is cash in because the organization has sold off assets.

Net changes in Current Liabilities gives you just the opposite result because if the net change to a Liability is positive, it means that you have borrowed money, which gives you more cash, and if the net change is negative, it means you have reduced debt by paying cash out.

Depreciation is always cash in if the organization is profitable. Example: If for the period you had $100,000 in Revenue and claimed $10,000 in Depreciation expense, where is the $10,000? The $100,000 came in as cash or as an increase to Accounts Receivable, but no real dollars went out in the form of cash or an increase to Accounts Payable to cover the Depreciation. Depreciation is one of the adjustments in the Accounting Cycle for allocating fixed assets, called a paper expense. The $10,000 is retained in the company and should be set aside to recoup the original investment.

When these three sets of accounting transactions are summed, the answer reports the net change in cash from operations.

2. Cash Flow from **Investing** refers to the purchase of Fixed Assets. When Fixed Assets are purchased it always represents cash out. It is true that some purchases are made on credit; however, that is offset by borrowing. The selling of Fixed Assets is cash in.

3. Cash Flow from **Borrowing** is more than just debt borrowing; it includes Equity borrowing. This may be a new concept for you; it is for many non-financial managers. Consumers generally believe that all borrowing is debt. For businesses, borrowing is any time you receive money and give an instrument of claim on the business's assets. In debt borrowing for the business, the claim is in the form of bonds, notes, commercial paper and mortgages. In Equity borrowing, the claim is in the form of Common Stock, Preferred Stock and Retained Earnings.

Note: Borrowing is any event where the business receives cash that the provider hopes to get back.

Debt borrowing is normally fixed, with fixed schedules, payments and interest. Equity borrowing is open ended and the stockholder may or may not receive anything in return; however, they expect to. In both cases the organization has received cash and given an instrument as proof of claim on its future benefits (Assets).

Debt borrowing brings cash in, while paying off principal is cash out.

Selling stock is cash in, while the payment of dividends or the repurchase of stock is cash out.

The final step is to sum the three parts of the Cash Flow Statement to determine net cash flow.

In summary, if the net cash flow is positive, it shows a net increase to your cash position (good). If on the other hand it is negative, it shows a net decrease of your cash position (very BAD). It is never good to be bleeding. There are times when it is necessary to reduce the organization cash balances, but it must be done with extreme caution. As mentioned earlier, of all the financial reports, many manufacturing executives consider this the most important. For them, it reports the real bottom line by answering the question, "Are you bleeding to death?"

Key Point Review (answers on page 163)

1. The Cash Flow Statement reconciles actual _____ .

2. Cash, which is the lifeblood of the business, is often called _____ .

3. Cash Flow Statements *cannot* measure _____ or the business's _____ .

4. Net increases to the change in Current Assets is cash _____ .

5. Net decreases to the change in Current Assets is cash _____ .

6. Net increases to the change in Current Liabilities is cash _____ .

7. Net decreases to the change in Current Liabilities is cash _____ .

8. Investing for a business is investing in _____ .

9. Borrowing includes both _____ and _____ .

10. Many managers of manufacturing facilities consider the _____ the most important.

Chapter 7:
Key Points and Terms

Accounting cannot tell you what must be done or give you facts about the future.

Accrual Accounting is an attempt by the Internal Revenue Service to prevent businesses from deferring taxable income to future periods. Revenue is earned when the customer receives benefit. Expenses cannot be claimed until consumed, even if paid for.

The accounting process, which has been around for as long as humans have had possessions, documents the past. This is important because learning from the past gives us insights to the future.

Non-financial managers must know three things:

1. Accounting must receive all required data about transactions on time or the financial report will be false, meaningless or even fraudulent.

2. Accounting cannot give any answers for the future, only facts about the past, which if understood will provide insights that will aid the decision maker in their decision-making process. The accounting process uses the Accounting Equation in the Accounting Cycle to generate the Balance Sheet, the Income Statement and the Cash Flow Statement. They, as outlined, provide documentation of the past, a foundation for understanding what has happened and insights to the future.

3. Accounting often becomes a battle of wits over taxes, instead of providing real information for decision makers. For example, the Balance Sheet is based on cost accounting and does not provide real information without footnotes.

In conclusion, accounting is very important because without an understanding of the past, there can be no educated decision making for the future. The non-financial manager must understand, however, that the most accurate facts about the past cannot give you answers for the future, only insights.

Key Terms:

Accounting – An arduous process for documenting the past

Accounting Cycle – The six-step process of accounting

Accounting Equation – The formula for double-entry accounting

Accounting Transactions – Business activities that can be readily measured in monetary terms

Accounts – The classifications of the General Ledger that the transactions are posted to

Accounts Receivable – Money owed to the company from the customers for credit purchases

Accrual Accounting – The process of accounting for benefits delivered and consumed

Adjusting Entries – Entries made at the end of the period for paperless transactions

Assets – The future benefits at cost which are reported on the Balance Sheet

Balance Sheet – The financial statement that reports future benefits and claims

Borrowing – Obtaining money and giving an instrument (bonds/stocks) as proof of claim

Capital Assets – A term applied to the Fixed Assets

Capital Stock – A term which identifies the money borrowed for stock issued

Cash – Real dollars

Cash Accounting – The accounting process for dollars received and spent

Cash Flow Statement – Tracks dollars in and dollars out

Chart of Accounts – The Table of Contents for the General Ledger

Circulating Capital – The life blood of the business; cash

Claims – The equities of the business; Liabilities and Owner's Equity

Cost – The actual purchase price

Cost Basis – The book value for tax purposes, usually the purchase price minus depreciation

Cost of Goods Sold – A composite of all expenses directly associated with inventory sold

Credit – A term in accounting meaning right, applied to the right side of an account

Current Assets – Future benefits that are going to be used up or turned over within one year

Current Liabilities – All debts due and payable within one year

Debit – A term in accounting meaning left, applied to the left side of an account

Depreciation – The allocating for benefits consumed of Fixed Assets over several years

Earnings per Share – The reporting of Net Income per share of Capital Stock outstanding

Equities – Claims against the future benefits (Assets) as reported on the Balance Sheet

Equity – Claims of the owners

Expenses – Dollars owed/paid of benefits consumed as reported on the Income Statement

Extraordinary Items – Expenses not a function of normal operations

Fee Appraisal – A professional real estate appraisal

Fiscal Year – The twelve-month accounting year of a company: like June 1 to May 31

Fixed Assets – All non-Current Assets

Future Benefits – Assets that can be consumed in a future period

General Journal – The book of original entry, in which all accounting transactions are recorded

General Ledger – The book of accounts, in which all transactions are posted to proper accounts

Income Statement – A primary financial statement which reports the exchange of benefits

Intangible Fixed Assets – Paper Assets like goodwill, patents and copyrights

Inventory – Future benefits (Current Assets) to be sold to customers

Investing – For businesses, investing is the purchasing of Fixed Assets

Liabilities/debt – Claims of the creditors

Long-term Debt – All non-Current Liabilities

Marketable Securities – A short-term holding place for cash

Matching Principle – The matching of benefits consumed with benefits provided

Net Income/Net Earnings – The net exchange of benefits, called Profit/Loss

Net Sales/Net Revenue – Total Revenue minus allowances, returns, uncollectibles, etc.

Non-financial Manager – Any manager not working or trained in finance or accounting

Operating Expenses – All normal expenses of doing business except Cost of Goods Sold

Operations – The normal functions necessary for business to operate

Owner's Equity – The claims of the owners

Permanent Accounts – Accounts that carry forward into future periods on the Balance Sheet

Prepaid Items – Current Assets that are prepaid future benefits like liability insurance

Profits – The net exchange of benefits (not dollars)

Profits/Loss (P&L) – The net exchange of benefits as reported on the Income Statement

Retained Earnings – Net Income from previous period reinvested in the business for owners

Revenue – Dollars earned/received for benefits provided

Sinking Fund – A holding place for cash that will not be used within one year

Stockholder's Equity – The claims of the owners

Supplies – Future benefits (Current Assets) that are used during daily operations

T Accounts – An accounting tool used to classify accounts in Step 1 of the Accounting Cycle

Tangible Fixed Assets – Real Fixed Assets like buildings, vehicles and equipment

Temporary Accounts – Accounts that must be reset to zero every period; Revenue & Expenses

Total Revenue – All contract sales, even if they are cancelled later

Trial Balance – Adding all Debit entries vs. Credit entries to ensure they are equal

Part II
Finance

Chapter 1:
Financial Analysis

Finance takes on three primary functions within a business: The Financing of Assets, Financial Analysis and Auditing.

The **Financing of Assets** (called **Borrowing**) has three parts: Short-term Debt, Long-term Debt and Equity. For a more in-depth discussion, refer to a college textbook on finance.

Short-term Debt (Current Liabilities) is primarily **Trade Credit**. Trade credit is the short-term financing of business purchases. When applied to your purchases it is called Accounts Payable and when applied to your customer's purchases from you it is called Accounts Receivable. Additional short-term financing may include: bank loans, short-term business IOUs called **Commercial Paper**, financing of Accounts Receivable called **Factoring** and lines of credit. Remember, short-term means that it is to be repaid within one year.

Long-term Debt for publicly traded corporations is financed through the sale of bonds and debentures, although it includes, especially for small businesses, the mortgaging of fixed assets and leases. Long-term borrowing is referred to as **Capital Budgeting** (see Chapter 6).

Equity borrowing is through the sale of **Common Stock**, **Preferred Stock** and the retention of earnings from the previous period called **Retained Earnings**. People ask, "How can this be borrowing?" The answer (as discussed in Part I, Chapter 6) is that the investors want to get their money back with a gain and they have a claim on the future benefits. There are just no fixed time lines or interest rates.

Debt borrowing is given legal precedence in the liquidation of the business; however, the owners still have a claim and want to get their money back. The relationship between debt and equity is called the **Leverage Ratio**. The leverage ratio and the current ratio are two of the most important ratios. The leverage ratio looks at long-term health, and the current ratio looks at short-term health.

Note: Understanding the Financial Analysis process is a key to success.

Financial Analysis is the process of evaluating the actual accounting transactions of the past to gain insights about future decisions. All decisions are guesses. As defined in the Introduction, the purpose of financial analysis is to make them educated guesses. Remember, accounting only records past transactions that can be measured in dollars. To have really educated guesses you must also include analysis of the non-accounting activities. (See Part III, Chapters 1 and 2.)

Financial Analysis can tell decision makers a lot about their financial decisions, such as inventory turnover, Accounts Receivables policies, spending on expenses and their ability to survive the short run.

Note: The Analysis process must be extended to all business activities.

Auditing, which gets a bad name because of tax audits, is an effective tool for improving the future. Many businesses have internal auditors or at least perform internal audits. Financial auditing tends to focus on the accuracy of the system, because there are right answers and the need to report financial information fairly under the rules of **GAAP** (Generally Accepted Accounting Principles). In the 21st century, however, auditing has expanded to include all activities and processes. The non-financial processes are constantly being improved with new technology and the development of new procedures. Managers and staff need to take a proactive look at auditing as a tool for improving the future.

Good internal auditing will find mistakes, inconsistencies, errors and shortcomings in the process. These events are generally caused by inadequacies in the process, or from shortages of time or resources, not from human failure. Even when it is from human failure, it is generally due to the lack of practice necessary to develop the proper skill sets.

Good managers learn from audits, called **Lessons Learned**, and use the information to develop better processes, called **Best Practices**. See Part III, Chapter 2 for a discussion of the controller's role in the 21st century as the manager's aid in improving the process.

In summary, remember you cannot change the past, you can only understand it, live and make corrections in the present and guess and improve the future. Financial information, when used as a management tool, provides the non-financial manager with a guide for their decision making (guessing).

Key Point Review (answers on page 163)

1. Trade Credit (accounts receivable and accounts payable) is not a function of accounting; it is a function of _____.

2. Comparing credit borrowing and equity borrowing in ratio form is called the _____.

3. Equity financing is borrowing because_____.

4. _____ borrowing has precedence in a liquidation.

5. _____ is when you borrow against your Accounts Receivable.

6. Planning for long-term debt it called _____ budgeting.

7. The sale of stock is _____.

8. The purpose of financial analysis is to help you make_____.

9. Good auditing allows managers to learn from the past, called _____.

10. Good auditing helps managers develop better processes, called _____.

Chapter 2:
Ratio Analysis

Ratio Analysis, when done properly, is a very powerful tool, providing the user with an in-depth understanding of what has been done. Good ratio analysis, when focused on **Trends**, can be used to aid in planning the future through forecasting and budgeting. The problem arises when managers put too much confidence in the numbers produced by ratios. The future is undefined, all plans and decisions are guesses and even the use of very good ratios does not change the uncertainty.

Non-financial managers need to focus on the non-financial ratios of productivity, customer satisfaction, employee retention, absenteeism or any other opportunity to create a ratio and then track the trends.

Weather forecasters have over 100 years of information, Doppler radar for accurate current information and highly trained experts, and yet, how accurate is a five-day weather forecast? In business, the weather is just one of the many variables. Managers should use ratios, but they must understand their limitations. A good **Forecast** is information (See Part III, Chapter 3) about the future; it is not just numbers.

This chapter will outline financial ratio analysis and then explain how the **Non-financial Manager** can use ratio analysis to go beyond the limitations of financial information.

Financial ratio analysis focuses on numbers from your accounting records which only include the accounting transactions. Financial ratio analysis is generally separated into five areas: **Liquidity Ratios**, **Leverage Ratios**, **Efficiency Ratios**, **Operating Ratios** and **Profitability Ratios**. Each ratio plays an important role in understanding past operations, which gives the decision maker insights to the future. For an in-depth understanding of financial ratios it is best to consult a good college textbook.

In general, ratio analysis simply sets two numbers into a ratio and then tracks the trends. The trends are more important than the numbers. The numbers only tell you what happened in the past, whereas, the trends show which direction you are heading in the future. If the trends are moving in the direction you want, it is good; if not, it gives you insights about areas that need your attention.

Current Ratio example							
Current Assets	=	$55,400	=	2.8	.8	= 40%	Red Flag
Current Liabilities		$19,500		1	2		
Industry Average is 2				With + or – 10% is good – Green Flag			

Illustration II-2-1

The **Current Ratio**, which is a Liquidity Ratio and one of the most important ratios, will be used here as a model for explaining the Ratio Analysis process (see Illustration II-2-1). First you identify the components which make up the ratio. For the Current Ratio they are Current Assets and Current Liabilities. This ratio explains why the Balance Sheet is divided into five parts. Current Assets are those assets that are going to be used up or turned over within one year. Current Liabilities are those debts which are due and payable within one year. When they are put into the Current Ratio, which is Current Assets divided by Current Liabilities, they help determine the liquidity of the organization. The bottom line here is, can you liquidate your Current Assets and cover your Current Liabilities? If you can, that means that you are solvent in the short run and you have one year within which to work on liquidating Fixed Assets at the best price. If, however, you cannot, it means that to pay off all your Current Liabilities you will have to liquidate some of your Fixed Assets. If you are forced to sell them too quickly, you will be forced to take losses, which could wipe out your equity and cause bankruptcy. This is why successful managers watch the Current Ratio very closely; if it is OK, then you have one year's breathing room.

When put into the formula, Current Assets minus Current Liabilities equals **Net Working Capital** or the amount of cash that you could generate if you liquidated the Current Assets and paid off the Current Liabilities. If this number is less than the industry standards, you are considered at high risk and functionally bankrupt. More simply, you just do not have the resources to survive the short run, like the athlete who is physically very healthy, but just too tired to run another one hundred yards.

Note: Businesses must be concerned about endurance, which is a function of Cash Flow.

The Current Ratio in Illustration II-2-1 is 2.8 to 1. The question to be asked is, is it good or bad? The general rule of thumb is that plus or minus 10% is good. You may ask, 10% of what? It is best to use the industry averages, but if you have none, start with your actual or desired trends. The industry averages are published by many sources: Dun & Bradstreet, the RMA used by banks, Moody's, the stock exchanges and others. The finance staff determines the best industry averages available for the key business ratios. For example, the industry average for the jewelry industry's Current Ratio is 2.0 to 1.

Note: This book is for non-financial managers so how to obtain these industry standards is not provided here; however, if you need to obtain any of these industry standards ask your financial officer or Certified Public Accountant (CPA).

Once you have determined the industry average of 2.0, you divide the variance of .8 (2.8 – 2.0) by it as follows: .8 divided by 2.0 equals 40%. This exceeds the plus or minus 10% so you red flag it. You then repeat this process for all important ratios. Green flag the ones that are within plus or minus 10% and red flag the ones that exceed plus or minus 10%.

The ones that are within the 10% are OK. You want to spend your time analyzing the red flagged ones. For the financial ratios you can seek the aid of your CPA or financial staff. For all the other critical ratios you can seek aid from your Controller. This process is performed every reporting period for all financial business ratios by the financial staff. The non-financial manager does not have to know how to analyze the ratios; they only have to know how to identify the red flagged ones. Then the financial staff or the Controller can provide the interpretation. Over time, each manager will learn about those ratios applicable to them.

Non-financial managers must look beyond the financial ratios, however. Remember, financial ratios are based on accounting transactions, which represent only a small portion of the business's activities. Ratio analysis can be used for anything that can be quantified, such as number of units produced over time or accident-free days.

To inspire creative ratio analysis, consider a school district's truancy department with a truancy problem. When it's bad, they need many truant officers out; otherwise, only a few. How do they know when it's likely to be bad? Well, for example, assume that they have observed that a large number of students pass through the intersection of 25th and Main each school day between 7 and 8 a.m. And they have also observed that if the number of children wearing red versus all other colors exceeds 1 to 2 it will be a high truancy day. Why? It's not important, although they would analyze it. It may be true that people who wear red generally get into more trouble, but it doesn't matter. The school district has learned over time that if the ratio exceeds 1 to 2 they need to get their truant officers out there because most of the time they will be needed.

> **Note:** Non-financial managers, with the aid of the Controller, need to find the ratios that give them insights for their decisions, even if they do not make sense to others. *This is one of the most important guides to decision making.*

In summary, the future is unknown; all decisions are guesses. Ratio analysis provides insights to the decision-making process and increases the probability of success.

Key Point Review (answers on page 163)

1. Good Ratio Analysis should focus on _____.

2. All plans, budgets and decisions are_____.

3. Ratio Analysis is much more than just _____.

4. Ratio Analysis simply sets_____ into a_____.

5. The Current Ratio is one of the most important because it measures short-term _____.

6. If you are not able to remain solvent in the short-term, you are considered _____.

7. Non-financial managers must look beyond_____.

8. Financial ratios only look at the accounting _____ , not at all business activities.

9. Finding the right ratio is one of the important parts of developing_____.

10. The Leverage Ratio monitors the business's_____.

Chapter 3:
Breakeven Analysis

Breakeven Analysis has two primary functions which are: To determine quantity necessary for breakeven or the price necessary for breakeven. The method used depends on the quality of the forecast and the flexibility of the price at which the product/service can be offered. Model 1 will assume that the price and costs are known and fixed. Model 2 will assume that the forecasted units to be sold are fixed.

Model 1 is for smaller businesses or businesses in very open markets where market share constraints are not a factor, markets where the business is basically able to sell more products or services than they can provide, called **Seller's Market**.

Model 1 starts by determining the selling price, the fixed cost and the variable cost. For Model 1 (see Illustration II-3-1) the selling price is set at $695, the fixed cost is set at $1,335 and the variable cost is $250 per unit. The formula shows mathematically that the Breakeven is at 3 units.

Numbers for breakeven

Our breakeven formula becomes

$695X	=	$1.335 + $250X

Where:

$695X	=	total revenue produced by selling X items
$1,335	=	total fixed costs
$250X	=	total variable costs incurred by producing X items

To solve:

$695X	=	$1,335	+	$250X
$445X	=	$1,335		
X	=	3		

To check:

$695(3)	=	$1,335	+	$250(3)
$2,085	=	$1,335	+	$750
$2,085	=	$2,085		

Illustration II-3-1

Variable Costs are costs that can effectively be assigned to a single unit of sale/production, like the door on a refrigerator or the tires on an automobile.

Fixed Costs are those that are shared by more than one unit of sale/production, like electricity, maybe snow removal or **Overhead**. The fixed costs are fixed over a number of units, but do change because of resource limitations. Example: In the service industry a customer service representative may on the average be able to handle 10 calls an hour. If the **Billable Time** of the clerk is $40 per hour then the fixed cost for 1 to 10 calls per hour is $40 and for 11 to 20 calls per hour is $80.

Note: Remember, Breakeven is about the future, so all estimates must include a consideration of probabilities and if the Costs could change.

Illustration II-3-2 assumes that the fixed cost of $1,335 is for 1 to 5 units, at which point additional resources are needed. This line is called the **Fixed Cost Line**. To this you add the variable costs at the rate of $250 per unit. This second line, which combines fixed costs and variable costs, is called the **Total Cost Line**.

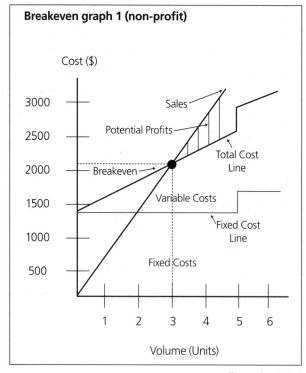

Illustration II-3-2

Next the sales figures are plotted at $695 per unit. This line is simply called Sales. Where the Sales and Total Cost lines intersect at 3 units is breakeven for a non-profit. At this point the sales have covered costs. The diverging area labeled potential profit represents the profits that additional sales should generate for a for-profit business.

For-profit businesses have an additional cost that can be included in breakeven called **Economic Cost**, normal profit or the cost of equity capital (the money borrowed from the owners). The return on equity is not an expense to be shown on the income statement or included in fixed or variable cost, but it is a cost of doing business. Illustration II-3-3 assumes that the owner's equity is $1000 and the desired return on equity is 20%, which results in a desired $200 in profits. In spite of what many people think, profitability is a function of equity, not revenue. The $200 is added to the fixed costs and the Fixed and Total Cost lines are adjusted. The breakeven is now 4 units. The for-profit must make at least four sales to breakeven, which includes a reasonable profit/Economic Cost.

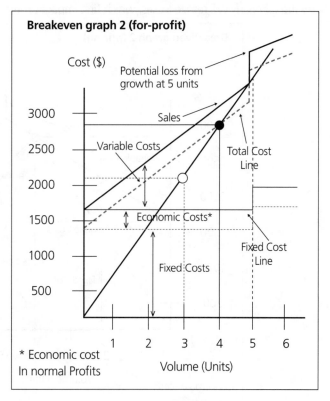

Illustration II-3-3

The question then asked is, "Will the market allow you to make four sales and what must be done to do it?"

Model 2 is often used by bigger businesses, where market share puts constraints on the number of sales that can be anticipated. Model 2 starts with the forecast. (See Part III, Chapter 3 for a discussion of the forecasting process.) Illustration II-3-4 assumes that the forecast is for 4 units. This sets the **Economy-of-Scale**, which is very important when dealing with large numbers. The costs per unit, for example, would be very different for 1,000 units versus 1,000,000 units. Once the forecast and economy-of-scale are set, the costs associated with each function of the business are broken into fixed and variable costs. Illustration II-3-4 assumes that the total, which includes Economic Costs (profits), is $2,765. Where the vertical line from 4 units intersects the horizontal line from $2,765 is breakeven, or $2,765 divided by 4 is $695. If the products/services are sold for more than $695, the company will realize profits in excess of Economic Cost, and if they are sold for less than $695 the company will realize losses, which first impact profits.

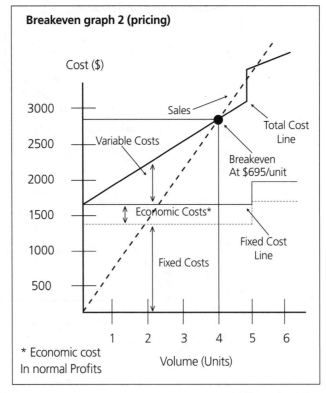

Illustration II-3-4

Breakeven analysis provides the foundation for the expression "Does the marginal benefit exceed the marginal cost?" In the 21st century this is the meaning of the term **Value Added**. Big business tracks this very closely, trying to ensure that each resource is pulling its own weight and providing more benefits than it consumes. That is the definition of Profits from Part I. Each employee must, however, ask themselves if they are really providing value added. One of the reasons for layoffs is that employees are wasting their time surfing the Net, on private phone calls or because they just don't understand that if a resource is not pulling its own weight it must be gotten rid of. Unfortunately, many good workers are caught in the layoffs and the slackers continue to run the company down.

> **Note:** It must be remembered that breakeven analysis is only a tool. It cannot give answers for the future, but if used properly it is a powerful guide which aids the decision maker in making educated guesses.

In summary, breakeven analysis is really used in every planning situation. In manufacturing it is called **Cost Accounting** or **Cost per Unit**. In project management the cost accounting is applied to activities or cost per activity (see Part III, Chapter 3, Forecasting). Individuals use it, for example, in determining what they will do on vacation to enjoy the best possible time with the available resources.

Key Point Review (answers on page 163)

1. Breakeven's two functions are to determine either_____ or _____.

2. Being able to sell more than you generate is called a _____.

3. Variable Costs are costs that can effectively be assigned to a _____.

4. Fixed Costs are those shared by _____.

5. Sales in excess of breakeven in Model 1 produce_____.

6. Economic Cost is the _____.

7. Economy-of-Scale is based on the number of_____.

8. Breakeven is reached when marginal _____ equals marginal _____.

9. When benefits provided exceed benefits consumed, it's called _____.

10. It must be remembered that Financial Analysis does not give answers, only

_____.

Chapter 4:
Time Line/Probability Analysis

Time is the problem! The present, that aspect of time within which you live, is but an instant. How well you perform in the present depends on how well prepared you are by the development of the correct skill sets. Management, however, is the future, which is unknown. All decisions, therefore, can only be guesses. Even a very precise manufacturing process may have its **Time Line** disrupted by worn bearings, which slow down the process; overheating, which warps the process; power failures, which stop the process; or human error.

In addition, in business, all the events affecting a sale cannot happen in the same instant, called The Present. The manager must understand that time lines are affected by what time of the year, month, week or day the events take place. It can make a big difference, because of surrounding circumstances, what day of the week and even what time of the day a meeting is held. Timing is most often the difference between success and failure in a stage play, in a football game, in a military action or in a business function. Two factors must be considered by the decision maker: The timing of the event and the probabilities associated with the event.

The Timing of Events (See Illustration II-4-1): This example considers the timing for some of the events that are necessary to meet a sales forecast. The solid line represents the Forecasted sales over a two year period in a rapidly growing company. This is the most critical line because every other function is a factor of this forecast. Any decisions, **Budgets** or activities that do not provide support and value added to this forecast are invalid by definition. This is hard for many new managers to understand. It is true that for-profit businesses would like to produce Profits; however, Profits are a function of Revenue, which is a function of customer satisfaction. Businesses would also like to provide a good work environment for employees, good retirement benefits and job security, and even support community events; all of these are also supported by Revenue as a function of the Forecast.

Taking a closer look at the illustration will demonstrate the previous statements. December of Year 1 has low Revenue and combined Expenses that are high, which would result in a loss (Sales of $35,000 and Total Expenses of $97,000). In fact, the 4th Quarter of Year 1 shows a loss because of rapid growth. To understand how businesses analyze these growth factors to deal with cash flow needs, please refer to the next chapter on **Pro Forma** analysis.

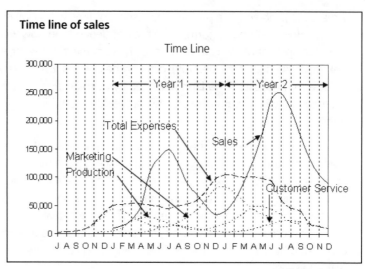

Time line of sales

Illustration II-4-1

> **Note:** In review, the purpose of a business is to meet the customer's needs. All functions and management decisions must answer the question, "What must be done and when must it be done to support the sales Forecast?"

To demonstrate the process, four key functions will be discussed: **Marketing**; **Production/ Service**; **Fixed Assets**; and **Customer Service**.

Marketing, which includes advertising, may incur many of its cost up to six months before the sale, as shown in the illustration. Advertising must be developed; television and radio time slots must be run. The problem here is that Accrual Accounting's **Matching Principle** says that the Expenses (benefits consumed) in a period must be matched with the Revenue (benefits provided) that the expenses are instrumental in generating within the period. The illustration, however, shows that the marketing expenses may not even be in the same year, much less the same quarter or month, of the sales that they are instrumental in supporting.

> **Note:** In a stable business, with constant annual sales, the Expenses and Revenues will average out annually. If the business has constant sales, however, it is often considered stagnant. In a rapidly growing company like the illustration, the matching principle becomes very confusing.

Production/Services generally happen before the sale, in the case of manufacturing, or after the sale, in the case of new home construction. Sometimes, as in the case of a haircut, it may happen at the same time as the sale; however, even fast food is not instantaneous.

Fixed Assets are necessary to produce a product or provide a service. These Fixed Assets generally have to be purchased and set up and staff trained on their use before the event. Even if you consider the simple event of going to a tennis match or any sports activity, the stadiums must be built well in advance of the event. Accrual Accounting tries to compensate for this with the use of depreciation, but what about the cost of financing, electricity, management planning time and use of human resources?

Customer Service takes place one to three months after the sale, as shown in the illustration.

It becomes clear very quickly that the use of modern day computers to bring accrual accounting down to a monthly perspective is futile. It may show accurately what has happened, but its use to project the future is problematical at best. Still it is all we have and if used with an understanding of its limitations it does provide insights for educated guessing (decision making).

Taking a closer look at the illustration will demonstrate the previous statements. November of Year 1 has low Revenue and high combined Expenses, which would result in a loss. In fact, the 4th Quarter of Year 1 shows a loss because of rapid growth. To understand how businesses analyze these growth factors to deal with cash flow needs, please refer to the next chapter on **Pro Forma** analysis.

The illustration demonstrates the absurdity of owners or stockholders that expect profits every year, quarter or month. If the business, including service businesses, is showing a profit every quarter there can be little or no growth. Likewise, if the business is in a rapid state of growth, where do the profits come from? The answer is future periods.

An in-depth understanding of this subject requires graduate-level study in Managerial Finance. It is enough, however, for the non-financial manager to simply be aware of the fact that things do not happen instantaneously. The most important guide to successful decision making is the understanding of time lines.

Probabilities are associated with Events: All events involving the future have uncertainty associated with them; therefore, all decisions, proposals, forecasts and budgets are subject to probability. *There are no facts about the future.* Many people try to rebut this with generalities like what about the sun rising each morning, a week has seven days, or 1 plus 1 equals 2. Well, what about them? Someday the sun will be gone, maybe not in your lifetime, but who knows? The calendar has changed many times throughout history and it may change again. As for 1 plus 1 equals 2, the author personally knows of efforts to take mathematics to a whole new level of understanding. So what? The question is not whether you can take the sun rising or 1 plus 1 equals 2 for granted; it is whether you can take the weather, customers, employees, the government, decisions, past successes, etc. for granted.

> **Note:** Just because something has worked in the past does not mean it is *guaranteed* to work in the future. Sometimes a random hunch is the best choice.

The decision maker must be prepared for change (See Part III, Chapter 6) and have contingency action plans ready. If there were no unexpected changes, managers would not be necessary. The business could program a computer to do it or just give it to an employee. The job of management is to manage, which is the phasing of the plan to reality, like a pilot adjusts the flight plan to weather and traffic changes in an effort to successfully reach their goal.

In summary, managers must put the timing and probability of events together for insights into their decision-making process.

Key Point Review (answers on page 164)

1. Time is the biggest problem because it is the _____.

2. One problem is that all of the events affecting a sale do not happen at the

   _____.

3. The timing of events are plotted on a _____.

4. All functions are based on the Time Line of the _____.

5. Profits, a function of revenue and expenses, are not necessarily _____.

6. A problem with Accrual Accounting is that the business may be in a _____.

7. A business always showing profits demonstrates _____.

8. All events have _____.

9. There are no _____ about the future.

10. For good insights into decision making, managers must consider the _____

    and _____of events.

Chapter 5:
Pro Forma Analysis

Pro Forma is a five-year look into the future. Pro Forma is often misused to mean only a five-year forecast of the Income Statement. The proper use of Pro Forma involves much more. This chapter discusses Pro Forma as used by managers as an effective financial tool in their decision-making process.

Pro Forma is a five-year projection of the three primary financial statements: **The Income Statement**, the **Balance Sheet** and the **Cash Flow Statement**.

The **Projected** Income Statement looks at Revenues to be earned and Expenses to be incurred over the next five years. All too often it is created by using the information from past Income Statements and mathematically projecting the numbers into the future. This does give the decision maker something to look at and it is easy to create with modern day computers, but it is meaningless and incorrectly called a forecast.

The forecast is the projected number of units of product or service to be delivered, along with the activities and resources necessary to provide them (see Part III, Chapters 3 and 4). A proper Projected Income Statement takes a lot of work and is the result of the conversion of valid five-year forecasts and budgets into the Income Statements. Small business owners and the owners of start-up businesses often ask bankers how they're supposed to know what is going to happen five years from now. The banker's response is: "Then why should I believe that you will be able to repay the loan?"

> **Note:** The future is a guess and it requires good information to be an educated guesser. If the Projected Income Statement is only based on the numbers using some accounting program's forecasting or budgeting features, it is no better than a five-day weather forecast.

WARNING: Even a properly prepared Projected Income Statement is a trap if it is not properly accompanied by the Projected Balance Sheet and Cash Flow Statement. Many businesses have literally sold themselves out of business. The question that must be answered is: "Will the business have the resources, broken down by month, to sustain the projected operations?"

The Projected Balance Sheet reflects the drain on assets and the use of debt borrowing in relation to the drain on Equity. In growth environments, the organization must generally obtain the assets necessary to support the increasing sales before the actual sales take place. In addition, it may then be some time before the Revenue is actually collected. How will this be financed and what are the time lines? It must be done through borrowing, debt and/or Equity.

> **Note:** The projected equity, however, is in the form of profits, which are in the form of Accounts Receivable.

Problem: The borrowing of debt and/or Equity is necessary before the sales, and profits are not realized until after. In addition, there is the problem of cash flow because profits do not reflect cash received. In order to determine required cash flow time lines, however, there must be valid projected Income Statements and Balance Sheets.

The Projected Cash Flow Statements are the key to success. It is very important to meet the forecast and manage the budget, but without adequate cash the business cannot function. The problem comes from the timing of cash flow shortages. Organizations have seasonal trends, as do their customers. The poor cash flow periods of their customer may negatively impact Accounts Receivable and delay cash receipts just when your organization has the greatest cash needs. A good Projected Cash Flow Statement identifies the timing of the expected receipt of cash from sales and the timing of actual cash payments to set up time lines, which identify cash shortages and surpluses.

Now the organization can take steps to plan the financing of its critical cash flow shortages. Quite often this is accomplished through the use of lines of credit based on receivables. As previously mentioned, cash flow management is considered the most important function by many managers, especially managers of production facilities. If the business has adequate cash flow it can handle just about anything. An effective cash flow projection should be done monthly, for at least the first two years, showing how cash shortages will be covered.

In summary, the Pro Forma provides the decision maker with The What, The How and The Way. The projected Income Statements outline "The What" in Revenue (benefits provided) and Expenses (benefits consumed). The projected Balance Sheets outline "The How" in Assets (future benefits) and Claims (debt and equity borrowing). And the Projected Cash Flow Statements outline "The Way" in real cash in, cash out and how cash flow shortages will be handled. Combined, they form the basis of the non-financial manager's guide to decision making.

Key Point Review (answers on page 164)

1. Pro Forma is a five-year projection of the three primary_____ .

2. The Projected Income Statement must be more than just a _____ .

3. The Projected Income Statement must be based on the _____ , not dollars.

4. A good Projected Income Statement is based on the conversion of valid _____ and_____ .

5. Even a properly prepared Income Statement could be a _____ .

6. The Projected Income Statement must be supported by projected_____ and_____ .

7. There is a problem of_____ when profits do not reflect cash received.

8. _____ are one of the keys to success.

9. Another problem is that, just when you need cash, it may be_____ .

10. The Pro Forma, when properly completed, provides the decision maker with _____ .

Chapter 6:
Capital Budgeting

Capital Budgeting is a term applied to the projected purchases of Fixed Assets because the costs and benefits must be projected over many years. This chapter will discuss three methods used to evaluate capital purchases, and presents the 21st century change. In the past, Capital Budgeting was focused on cash out, cash in and the dollar returns on investments in Fixed Assets. In the 21st century the focus is on Value Added. The methods to be discussed are: Payback, Net Present Value, Internal Rate of Return and Value Added. All four methods will use the two investment possibilities represented in Illustration II-6-1.

Two projects for investment

Payback

Many small businesses use this method, while most large corporations do not. Its popularity is due to its simplicity and sensitivity to the fact that many small businesses don't have a lot of capital.

This method simply determines the number of years required to pay back an investment.

Project A	**Project B**
Cost = $100,000	Cost = $100,000
Expected future cash flow:	Expected future cash flow:
Year 1 $50,000	Year 1 $100,000
Year 2 $50,000	Year 2 $5,000
Year 3 $110,000	Year 3 $5,000
Years 4 and after: None	Years 4 and after: None
Total = $210,000	Total = $110,000
Payback = 2 years	Payback = 1 year

Illustration II-6-1

Payback is the easiest method to use which is the primary reason for its popularity. It determines, based on anticipated cash flows, which investment will recoup the cash invested in the shortest period of time so that it can be reinvested. There is merit to this when the focus is on cash turnover. The problem is that it does not take into account the Time Value of Money. The illustration shows that the proposed investment, in both cases, is $100,000, which will be recouped in two years using Investment A and in one year using Investment B. Applying the Payback method, the decision would be to go with Investment B.

Net Present Value looks at the Time Value of future cash flows discounted back to **Present Value**. It answers the question, "Which would you rather have: $1,000 today or $1,000 a year from now, assuming an 8% investment opportunity?" Today of course, because you could invest it at the 8% and at the end of the year it would be worth, called **Future Value**, $1,080. The Net Present Value method just reverses the process and asks the question, "What is $1,000 to be received one year from now worth in today's dollars, called Present Value?" The answer is found by discounting the $1,000 using the same 8%, called **Cost of Capital** and the time value tables found in the back of all accounting textbooks. This example uses the Present Value of a Dollar table as shown in Illustration II-6-2. The decision maker looks at one period for one year at 8%, the discount rate, and finds the factor, which in this case is .926. This factor of .926 is then multiplied times the Future Value of $1,000, which gives you a Present Value of $926. This means that if you invested $926 today at 8% interest, in one year it would be worth $1,000.

Present value of a dollar table

Periods	6%	7%	8%	9%	10%	11%	12%	20%	30%	40%
1	0.043	0.935	0.926	0.917	0.909	0.901	0.893	0.833	0.769	0.714
2	0.890	0.873	0.857	0.842	0.826	0.812	0.797	0.694	0.592	0.510
3	0.840	0.816	0.794	0.772	0.751	0.731	0.712	0.579	0.455	0.364
4	0.792	0.763	0.735	0.708	0.683	0.659	0.636	0.482	0.350	0.260

Illustration II-6-2

Net Present Value, however, takes this another step. The decision maker would then subtract the investment of $909, leaving a net of $27 called Net Present Value. This means that the investment will return the required 8% plus an additional $27. In general, any investment that has a positive Net Present Value is good.

Applying Net Present Value to the two investment opportunities using a 12% Cost of Capital (discount rate) (see Illustration II-6-3), the decision maker determines that the Net Present Value of investment A is $62,820, while the Net Present Value of investment B is a negative, shown in parentheses, ($3,155). Using the Net Present Value method, Investment A is clearly better.

Net Present Value

Also known as discounted cash flow, this method takes into account the "time value of money," using a technique known as "discounted present value." This method compares the present value of the expected future benefits of a project to the present value of the expected cost of the project.

$$NPV = PVB - PVC$$

where
NPV = net present value
PVB = present value of benefits
PVC = present value of costs

If NPV is positive, accept
If NPV is negative, reject

Project A

Assume a 12% discount rate:

PVB_A = [$50,000] [_____] + [$50,000] [_____] + [$110,000] [_____]

PVB_A =

PVB_A =

Project B

Assume a 9% discount rate:

$NPV_B = PVB_A - PVC_A$

NPV_B = [$100,000] [0.917] + [$5,000] [0.842] + [$5,000] [0.772] − $100,000

NPV_B = $91,700 + $4,210 + $3,860 − $100,000

NPV_B = ($230)

Illustration II-6-3

Note: All methods of Capital Budgeting are only as good as the estimated cash flows from depreciation, salvage or sale of assets, etc.

Internal Rate of Return is basically the same as Net Present Value, except that the Cost of Capital figure is unknown so a series of trial and error calculations must be used. In the example of $1,000 cash to be received in one year, it was assumed that the Cost of Capital (discount rate) was 8% and the investment was $909, which produced a Net Present Value of $27. The question is: What is the Internal Rate of Return or how much could you afford to pay for the Cost of Capital?

Using the Internal Rate of Return method, the decision maker must use trial and error and guess at the correct percentage rate. For this example, the decision maker first tries 9%. Looking at the table, the decision maker finds that the factor is .917 and multiplies it times the $1,000 to get a Present Value of $917; then subtracts the investment of $909 to get a Net Present Value of $8. This tells the decision maker that the Internal Rate of Return is more than 9%. So the decision maker tries again using 10%. This time the factor is .909. Multiplying it times the $1,000, the Present Value is $909, then subtracting the investment of $909, the Net Present Value is zero. This tells the decision maker that the Internal Rate of Return is 10%. Very seldom will it come out exactly like this example. In the real world, the decision maker just uses trial and error to get reasonably close.

Internal Rate of Return

The Internal Rate of Return (IRR) is the discount rate which would bring the present value of the benefits to equal the present benefits of the cost.

General decision rule for IRR—Any project with an IRR greater than or equal to the firm's cost of capital should be accepted. If IRR is less than the firm's cost of capital, the project should be rejected.

Project A

Assume a 20% discount rate:

$NPV_A = PVB_A - PVC_A$

$NPV_A = [\$50,000] [0.833] + [\$50,000] [0.694] + [\$110,000] [0.579] - \$100,000$

$NPV_A = \$41,650 + \$34,700 + \$63,690 - \$100,000$

$NPV_A = \$40,040$

Assume a 40% discount rate:

$NPV_A = [\$50,000] [0.714] + [\$50,000] [0.510] + [\$110,000] [0.364] - \$100,000$

$NPV_A = \$35,700 + \$25,500 + \$40,040 - \$100,000$

$NPV_A = \$1,240$

Project B

Assume a 9% discount rate:

$NPV_B = PVB_A - PVC_A$

$NPV_B = [\$100,000] [0.917] + [\$5,000] [0.842] + [\$5,000] [0.772] - \$100,000$

$NPV_B = \$91,700 + \$4,210 + \$3,860 - \$100,000$

$NPV_B = (\$230)$

Illustration II-6-4

Applying the Internal Rate of Return method to the two business examples (see Illustration II-6-4), you find that the Internal Rate of Return for Investment A is just over 40% and for investment B it is just under 9%. What does this mean? The decision maker, if making investment A, could go out and borrow the money necessary and pay Willy the Shark up to 40% for it and it would still be a good deal. Whereas, if they had to pay 9% for the money to be invested in B, they would pass.

Note: There are many other factors to be considered like Value Added; these examples only demonstrate the financial perspective.

Value Added is not really a model because it looks at the elusive benefits that cannot easily be measured in dollars and are therefore not accounting transactions. The accounting-based model for Value Added would be breakeven analysis. Breakeven, while being a good starting point, is not enough. In the 21st century, decision makers are focusing on customer satisfaction, which includes many hard to measure benefits like goodwill. A company puts down new carpet, which improves employee morale, which improves productivity, which reduces expenses, which increases profitability, which produces a positive Net Present Value on the investment in the carpet. The problem is that this cannot be easily demonstrated in dollars and stuck into a mathematical model. The benefits are often very hard to identify and some negative person could argue whether the benefits even exist.

Using Value Added and applying it to Investment B, which had a negative Net Present Value of ($230), the decision maker may find that there are many non-direct cash flow benefits that impact the emotional responses of your customers and employees. Location, appearance, a real person answering the phone, advertising and training are just a few possibilities.

In summary, Capital Budgeting is an attempt to make educated guesses (decisions) about long-term capital investments. Value Added goes beyond the accounting transaction and tries to look at the dynamics of the whole picture in an effort to maximize results.

Key Point Review (answers on page 164)

1. Capital Budgeting is projected financing of _____ .

2. The Payback method determines which opportunities will _____ .

3. Payback does not account for _____ .

4. Present Value _____ future cash flows back to what it's worth today.

5. Net Present Value requires subtracting _____ from the Present Value.

6. Net Present Value results are considered good if _____ .

7. All methods of Capital Budgeting are based on _____ .

8. Internal Rate of Return uses_____ and_____ .

9. Internal Rate of Return tells you how much you could pay for the Cost of Capital and still have a _____ .

10. Value Added includes the _____ benefits not easily measured in dollars.

Chapter 7:
Key Points and Terms

Finance has three key functions: Financing of Assets, Financial Analysis and Auditing. This part has focused on Financial Analysis, which provides an understanding of the past. Too often, managers believe that Financial Analysis can project the future. *It cannot!*

Financial Analysis provides us with Lessons Learned, an understanding of the past that can be used to estimate the future. Good Financial Analysis aids non-financial managers in making educated guesses (decisions).

Non-financial managers must focus on three key points:

1. The trends provide the understanding, not the numbers. The trends show the direction of movement in a specific area that provides the insights about the future. Successful managers use the trends to phase their plans to reality.

2. The time lines outline the sequencing of events, which is critical for effective management. A sale or event does not happen in an instant. When preparing Thanksgiving dinner, the turkey must be thawed and stuffed before it is cooked. Understanding time lines may be the most important responsibility of managers.

3. The analysis process must extend beyond accounting transactions. The process must be extended to all business activities even if the benefits are not readily measurable in dollars and are hard to define. The key to ratio analysis is the insights that the numbers provide. Similar insights can be obtained about all business activities if the analysis process is properly applied.

In conclusion, the Financial Analysis process converts the documented facts of the past into usable information for the present, which provide insights to the future.

Key Terms:

Auditing – The process of systematically reviewing past activities

Best Practices – The educated guess (laws, plans, decisions) for the future

Billable Time/Rate – The hourly cost of consuming (using) a resource, normally employees

Borrowing – Obtaining money and giving an instrument (bonds/stocks) as proof of claim

Breakeven – The level of sales at which marginal benefits equal marginal costs

Budget – The projection of how the resources will be deployed to accomplish the Forecast

Capital Budgeting – The projecting of the purchasing of Fixed Assets

Commercial Paper – IOUs of corporation, normally short-term

Common Stock – The controlling ownership or the claim with the greatest risk

Cost Accounting – Tracking cost on a per unit or activity basis

Cost of Capital – The financing cost of Debt borrowing

Cost per Unit – The costing function of Cost Accounting

Current Ratio – The Liquidity Ratio which tracks short-term solvency

Customer Service – The activity of providing the customer support after the sale

Economic Cost – The financing cost of Equity borrowing, called normal Profits

Economy-of-Scale – Economic efficiencies in larger numbers of production

Efficiency Ratios – Ratios that report turnover as a function of Net Sales

Equity – Claims of the owners

Factoring – Debt borrowing against Accounts Receivable or the sale of Accounts Receivable

Financial Analysis – The mathematical analysis of accounting transactions

Financing of Assets – The borrowing (Debt or Equity) to invest in Assets

Fixed Assets – Assets that are necessary to produce a product or provide a service

Fixed Cost line – The line on a breakeven chart that represents the Fixed Costs

Fixed Costs – Costs that cannot be conveniently assigned to a single unit of production or sale

Forecast – The projections of The What (Scope) that make up the deliverables to the customer

Future Value – What a monetary value is worth at some time in the future

GAAP – Generally Accepted Accounting Principles

Internal Rate of Return – The Cost of Capital that will result in a zero Net Present Value

Lessons Learned – Your knowledge of the past about what is being done right and wrong

Leverage Ratio – The relationship between Debt and Equity borrowing

Leverage Ratios – Ratios that report on how heavily financed a business is

Liquidity Ratios – Ratios that report the short-term solvency of the business

Long-term Debt – All non-current Liabilities

Marketing – The function of defining customers' needs and selling them a product/service

Matching Principle – The matching of benefits consumed with benefits provided in a period

Net Present Value – The Present Value of future cash flow minus the investment

Net Working Capital – Current Assets minus Current Liabilities

Non-financial Manager – Any manager not working or trained in finance or accounting

Operating Ratios – Ratios that report expenses as a function of Net Sales

Overhead – General business expenses not associated with operations

Payback – A Capital Budget method focused on how quickly the investment can be recaptured

Preferred Stock – Equity borrowing that normally does not have a controlling interest

Present Value – The value of future dollars discounted to today's value

Pro Forma – A five-year projection of the three primary financial statements

Probabilities – The mathematical term applied to the future's uncertainty

Production/Service – Generally happens before the sale, as in the case of manufacturing, or after the sale, as in the case of new home construction

Profitability Ratios – Ratios that report the returns on investments

Projected – A term applied to the outlines of future events

Retained Earnings – Net Income that is reinvested on behalf of the owners

Seller's Market – When there are more buyers than products or services

Short-term Debt – Normally, debt that will be paid back within a year

Time Line – A look at the sequencing of the activities of an event

Total Cost line – The total of fixed cost plus variable cost plotted on a chart

Trade Credit – Short-term Debt used to finance business credit purchases

Trends – The line on a chart that shows changes over time

Value Added – When benefits provided exceed benefits consumed

Variable Costs – Those costs that can be directly related to a sale or unit of production

Part III
Controlling

Chapter 1: Management

You cannot manage or control the past; you can only record and understand it. You cannot manage or control the present; you can only act, and how well you act depends on your skill sets. All management and controlling is the future, which means that every decision is a guess; the purpose of accounting and finance is to make your decision making educated guessing. This chapter also will clarify the illusion of controlling.

Management is the process of modifying or phasing the plan to reality. Good management is not a function of how well you can follow a plan or budget; it is how well you can make them work in the uncertain reality of tomorrow. Tomorrow is unknown; trained weather forecasters with 100 years of documentation and Doppler radar cannot tell you what the weather will be five days from now with any guarantee. The weather is only one of the variables that managers must deal with in their decision making. Management is made up of three primary functions: **Planning**, **Contingency Planning** and **Controlling**.

This chapter will overview each of these. Chapters 3, 4 and 5 will discuss planning functions; Chapters 4 and 6 will discuss Contingency Planning and Chapter 2 will discuss Controlling and the functions of the Controller.

Planning is the process of using the understanding gained from the financial analysis of past documentation to create a plan that will guide you to your goal. A good example of this is when a pilot prepares a **Flight Plan** for a flight from New York to Los Angeles. The pilot takes into account routes, other air traffic, aircraft speed, flight restriction and the weather adjusted for the time of year such as blizzards over the Rocky Mountains, tornadoes in Kansas, severe storms over the Ohio River Valley and even hurricanes along the East Coast. Managers must do the same, being careful not to take anything for granted.

Taking things for granted often creates the biggest problems because the manager is not properly prepared to deal with them when they go wrong. It is, however, human nature to try to control processes and people by insisting that they produce the same results every time. *This is not rational.* Machinery wears out and breaks down. People get sick or just have a bad day. Even top professionals like Tiger Woods do not hit every ball as planned or win every tournament.

Note: To make plans based only on the facts of the past, without contingency planning for the reality of the present and the uncertainty of the future, is not good management.

Contingency Planning, which looks at change, risk and probability, is the heart and soul of successful management. If things did always go the way you planned, you would not need managers. In the example of the pilot and the flight across the United States, a major part of the Flight Plan is the contingencies: Alternate airports at which to land, fuel reserves, emergency procedures, alternate routes and emergency equipment like life vests. Few planes crash, but some do; the trick is to survive.

A successful manager (decision maker) is not someone who is lucky enough to have things go the way they planned. A successful manager is one who achieves their objective when normal things go wrong. The Value Added of good contingency planning is paid back through reduced problem solving. The problem is that if the contingency planning really works, the problems do not materialize for comparison. Once the plan, with contingencies, is in place, then the real job of management begins—controlling the operation to achieve the desired goal by reaching the destination successfully.

Controlling is the art of problem solving on the fly. Managers can only function in the present. They cannot change or control the past. That is already fixed. They cannot dictate or control the future that is the unknown realm of nature. Managers can only guide (control is really the wrong term) the events by having well-developed plans, contingencies and skill sets that allow them to act correctly in the present.

Pilots practice emergency procedures, athletes must practice and so must managers. Knowing what to do is not good enough. The manager must be able to do it within the split second, called The Present. Saying or doing the wrong thing, showing that they lack confidence, or not remembering the things to do is devastating for managers.

So why do people foolishly say "Those who can't do, manage"? Doing is simply a matter of mastering the skill sets through practice. Some people, because of natural ability, can do it better, but it is still just mastering a proven process. *Management, however, is mastering the number one fear of the human species—the fear of the unknown (change).* It takes a special kind of person to cope successfully with the constantly changing uncertainty of tomorrow.

Controlling is an illusion, a misuse of the language, because the past is written, the present is but a split second and the future is unknown. The term guiding, or maybe phasing, should be used. Every plan, every decision, is a guess. It is only people who are afraid of the unknown who try to pretend that they can control it. Your ability to plan, to make decisions, is only as good as your decision-making skill sets.

A skill set is something you can do well without thinking about it. What you know is not necessarily a skill set. To demonstrate, please sign your normal signature on this line:

_____

You can do it easily because you know who you are and you have practiced. Now sign your name again, using your other hand, on this line:

_____

This was not so easy even though you have the same knowledge. A skill set is not what you know, but what you can do well. In successful management (decision making) it is not what you think you know but what you can do that allows you to successfully guide your organization to its goal.

In summary, successful management is being able to develop good plans, identify contingencies and guide (control) **effectively** by developing the skill sets necessary to phase the plan to life's ever-changing mystery.

Key Point Review (answers on page 164)

1. Management is the process of _____ the plan to reality.

2. Management is made up of three functions: _____, _____ and_____ .

3. Managers must not take anything for _____.

4. Insisting on the same results dogmatically every time is not _____.

5. Contingency Planning considers_____ , _____ and_____.

6. A successful manager is one who achieves their goals even when _____.

7. Managers, like pilots and athletes, must _____.

8. Controlling is an illusion because you *cannot* dictate the _____.

9. Management is mastering the number one fear of the human species, which is

_____.

10. _____ might be a better term than controlling.

Chapter 2:
The Controller

This chapter provides a working understanding of the 21st century function of the Controller—which is not the same as the 20th century function of the Comptroller. It also will illustrate how the Controller aids managers and how managers can obtain value added from the Controller in their decision-making process.

The 20th century Comptroller was an advanced accountant. That position has given way to the Chief Financial Officer (CFO) and the Chief Accounting Officer (CAO). Modern day computerized accounting has really streamlined the accounting process.

What is a **Controller**? Well, what do you think of when you think of Controller? Maybe an Air Traffic Controller who provides information to pilots in their decision-making process as they fly. Maybe it is the central processing unit in your car, called a controller, that gathers information from sensors about oil pressure and engine temperature and reports this information through the dashboard to the driver in their decision-making process, as they attempt to reach their goal. Nearly everywhere the term Controller is used in the 21st century, it refers to individuals or devices that give information to decision makers. No longer is the information provided by good business Controllers limited to the financial information, which is based on only a limited number of business activities, called accounting transactions.

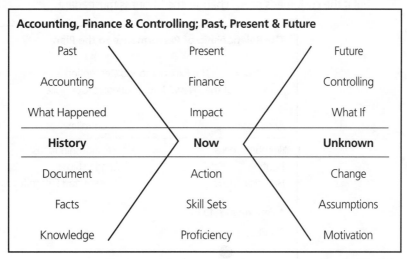

Accounting, Finance & Controlling; Past, Present & Future		
Past	Present	Future
Accounting	Finance	Controlling
What Happened	Impact	What If
History	**Now**	**Unknown**
Document	Action	Change
Facts	Skill Sets	Assumptions
Knowledge	Proficiency	Motivation

Illustration III-2-1

The 21st century Controller must stop living in the past and focus on the future. Illustration III-2-1 shows the relationships of accounting, finance and controlling (guiding). Accounting records the past, providing documentation and knowledge. Finance analyzes and interprets the historical accounting information and converts it into ratios and useful information to aid managers in their decision-making process. Controlling (management) is the future, which is defined by uncertainty, change and risk.

Note: Managers, like the pilot, need current, relevant information to aid in their guessing (decision making) as they work to guide the organization to a successful fulfillment of its goals.

The Controller's focus is on accomplishing the goal, the relationship of **Performance** to the plan. The key is in understanding what is meant by performance. Many people believe that this means comparing where they are in the process with the budget, but this is *not* correct. Performance is more than just where you are; it is where you are in terms of where the customer needs you to be (see Illustration III-2-2). This is then compared to the plan or budget. The plan/budget sets limitations on just how adaptable a business is to change; but if the customer's needs change, the business must adapt.

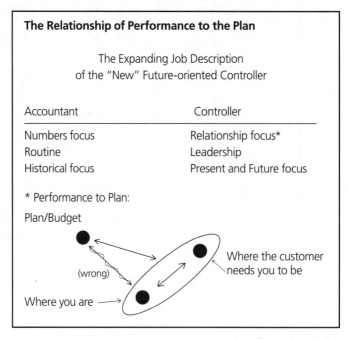

Illustration III-2-2

A problem that has arisen in many companies is that senior managers mistakenly believe that the Controller is still just part of the accounting function. They, therefore, hire accountants, whose natural focus is on the past, or Certified Public Accountants (CPAs) to be the Controller. Too often these Controllers focus on accounting as the only important information because that is what they understand. Good CPAs are above this and are able to focus on the bigger picture.

> *Note:* Remember, if you are only using accounting information (documentation from that past that only includes accounting transactions), your forecasts are no better than a five-day weather forecast.

What makes a good 21st century Controller?

It is the ability to provide **Timely Information** to managers for their decision-making (guiding) process. The key to this is the word timely. Decisions can only be made in the present; if delayed, the decision maker may miss the window of opportunity. Timely means that the Controller provides the best information possible when the decision maker needs it. If the decision maker does not need the information until 3 p.m. tomorrow, then the Controller should continue processing information and provide the best information at 3 p.m. tomorrow. The Controller should not just give them what they have today because the Controller is going to be busy tomorrow. On the other hand, if the decision maker must make the decision today, being told that they have to wait until tomorrow because the reports are not ready yet is *not* acceptable. By tomorrow, the decision maker may have missed the **Window of Opportunity**. Timely is the best information available when needed. After all, the decision is a guess and sometimes decisions must be made with no information. Besides, no information is better than bad information.

In summary, four functions highlight the modern day Controller's ability to do their job well: Knowing what information each decision maker needs, knowing how they are going to use it, knowing how to effectively gather the needed information and knowing how to effectively provide the information in a timely manner. In the 21st century the Controller is a provider of information, not an accountant.

Key Point Review (answers on page 164)

1. A Controller in the 21st century is someone who _____.

2. The function of the Controller is to provide _____.

3. Performance is defined as: Where are you in terms of where _____

    _____.

4. Decision makers must act within the _____.

5. A Controller must know what information each_____.

6. Plus the Controller must know how to effectively gather _____.

7. Plus the Controller must know how the information _____.

8. Plus the Controller must know how to provide information in a _____.

9. The 21st century Controller must stop living in the_____.

10. The focus of the 21st century Controller should be on the _____.

Chapter 3:
Forecasting

Forecasting is determining the number of units of product or service to be delivered in a certain period. This chapter begins by defining forecasting. Then it will give a basic model for organizational forecasting and finish with a working model for internal forecasting, which provides managers with a foundation for all **Budgeting**.

Forecasting is the process used in defining the deliverables (scope) that will meet the expectations of the stakeholders. The stakeholders could be customers, your boss, another department, taxpayers (the public) if you are putting a person on the moon, or your family if you are preparing Thanksgiving dinner. Forecasting is a function of Scope (deliverables), the bottom line of the Triple Constraint (see Chapter 5). Many managers put the cart before the horse and get involved with trying to determine how long it will take (Time) or how they will get it done (Resources), neither of which is relevant until they have a clear understanding of the stakeholders' expectations defined in **The What**, the **Quality** and the **Quantity**.

Many managers confuse forecasting with Budgeting, believing that they are forecasting if they forecast a budget. Forecasting and Budgeting are not the same and they are not accounting or financial activities. They are, respectively, marketing and management. In review, accounting records the past and finance interprets the past. Marketing, however, estimates what is to be done, at what quality and in what quantity (called **Forecasting**). Management then determines how it is to be done (called **Budgeting**) and works to get it done (called Controlling). Management and Controlling were discussed in Chapters 1 and 2 of Part III and Budgeting will be discussed in Chapter 4. This chapter focuses on forecasting, the defining of The What, The How Well and The How Many.

Forecasting begins at the organizational level. What departments and managers do is a function of the organization's forecast. Therefore, this chapter will give a basic outline of organizational forecasting and then a working forecasting model for departmental and manager levels. For a more in-depth understanding of forecasting, please read any college textbook on the fundamentals of marketing.

Organizational Forecasting

1. The *first step* is to identify the stakeholders (customers), their demographics and their need. Once you have defined the need of the stakeholders, you can create or find a product/service that will meet their need. The product/service for this example will be Widgets.

2. The *second step* is to define the geographic area, called **Workable Market**, that the business will be able to support, which answers the question: "Within how large an area, given your resources, can your business support the needs of your stakeholders?" This defined area may be a small town, your metropolitan city, your state or maybe, if it is a large company, the country or the world. This area should be clearly defined on a map, showing barriers and competition. If you take on too large an area and are unable to meet your stakeholders' demands, you put yourself at a high risk of failure. For this example we are going to use a metropolitan area like Minneapolis/St. Paul or Dallas/ Ft. Worth.

3. The *third step* is to make the actual forecast, which is determining how many Widgets you will sell/deliver (see Illustration III-3-1).

Organizational Forecasting Model

Step 1: Identify the stakeholders, their demographics and their need.
Identify the product or service: <u>Widgets</u>.

Step 2: Define the geographic area. <u>A metropolitan area</u> – Have outlined on a map.

Step 3: a. Determine the total market demand: <u>10,000,000 units</u>
      b. Calculate the forecast: 10,000,000 x 20% = <u>2,000,000 units</u>

Step 4: List the activities which must be performed and calculate cost.

Production	Marketing	Human Resources	Accounting	Customer Service
A $ 0000	A $00000	A $ 000000	A $0000	A $00000
B 00000	B 0000	B 0000	B 00000	B 0000
C 0000	C 000000	C 00000	C 0000	C 00000
D 00000	D 00000	D 0000	D 0000	D 0000
E 000000	E 0000	E 000	E 000	E 000
F 0000	F 000	F 0000	F 0000	F 000
$0000000	$0000000	$0000000	$0000000	$0000000 = $20,000,000

Determine economic cost   4,000,000

Forecasted minimum Revenue $24,000,000

Calculate minimum selling price $24,000,000/2,000,000 units = 12

Illustration III-3-1

You begin by determining the **Target Market** demand. For this example, the total demand is determined to be 10,000,000 Widgets or Widget substitutes. You then estimate your market share based on your understanding of your competition, available substitutes and other market information. It is determined that being a primary company in this market, your estimated markets share will be 20%, or 2,000,000 Widgets. You will notice that there are *no* dollar signs. The forecast is not a function of accounting, finance or dollars. The forecast is (in spite of the greed of the '80s and '90s) a function of deliverables to the stakeholders. From this point on every decision of management must be based on what it will take to produce, market, deliver and service 2,000,000 Widgets. If that number changes up or down then all plans and budgets must be adjusted.

Note: If an organization is using accounting programs to create dollar forecasts, the results are similar to a weather forecast, and you know how reliable they are.

---

4. The *fourth step* is to price your Widgets using **Breakeven**. This is done by defining the activities that must be performed by every department in your organization that are necessary for your organization to be able to produce, market, deliver and service 2,000,000 Widgets. This includes all supporting departments like Human Resources. You then estimate what it will cost each department to perform their functions (this process will be illustrated in our discussion of departmental forecasting). The sum total of these amounts is your cost (it should include all overhead) and represents the minimum that you must receive in revenue for your Widgets to breakeven (see information on breakeven analysis in Part II, Chapter 3). Let us say that, for this example, the total cost is $20,000,000. This means that a non-profit organization must generate $20,000,000 in revenue to breakeven, with a unit price of $10. For-profit organizations have an additional cost, called Economic Cost, which is normal profit. They have owners who require a return on their investment; it represents the cost of Equity (capital). You determine the cost of capital based on equity and add it to your cost. We have determined that your cost of capital is $4,000,000; therefore, your total revenue must be at least $24,000,000, or $12 per unit. If you do not receive at least $12 per unit, the owners will have their profits cut and may even lose money.

Note: The $24,000,000 is forecasted revenue, but it is not the forecast; the forecast is 2,000,000 Widgets.

Marketing now compares this $12 per Widget price with what the market will bear and with what competition is doing. If the market is not ready to pay $12 or competition is providing a similar product for less, then marketing develops an advertising strategy to educate your customers on why your Widgets are worth $12. Many people argue that you must cut the price; *this is ignorance*. If you cut the price, you cut profits or you must cut cost, which cuts quality. If you are the cheapest in town, then you are the cheapest in town. Real customers want a good product at a fair price. Cheap is a function of poor quality.

Departmental Forecasting

Now that you have your organization's forecast of 2,000,000 Widgets you can complete your departmental and manager forecasts. The process is virtually the same; the following, however, is going to convert it to a working model for managers. First you pick a department like Human Resources and follow the forecasting steps.

Steps 1 and 2 are easy; they are your organization (XYZ, Inc.). The remaining steps are placed in an Excel® spreadsheet (see Illustration III-3-2).

Human Resources Department

What	How many	Cost per activity	Total	Outsourcing cost per activity
Primary				
Hiring	50	$8,000	$40,000	$6,500
Performance reviews	300	$350	$105,000	
Etc.	xxx	$xxx	$xxx,xxx	$xxx
Other				
Filing	xxxx	$x	$xx,xxx	
Policies				
Change	xx	$xx	$xxx	$xxx
Compliance	xxx	$xxx	$xx,xxx	$xxx
Etc.	xxxx	$xx	$xx,xxx	

Total Forecasted Cost: $1,456,000

Illustration III-3-2

Column 1 lists **The What** (the deliverables, products or services) that your organization called Human Resources (HR) is to provide your stakeholder, XYZ, Inc., so that XYZ, Inc. will be able to produce, market, deliver and service 2,000,000 Widgets. These deliverables are called activities, and because there are so many of varying importance, you break them into two categories: Primary activities and Other activities. Primary activities are those few that take up most of the department's time and resources (reference the Pareto Principle, the 80/20 Rule). Other activities are the remaining miscellaneous activities. All the activities must be completed, of course, but if you have good controls on the 20% of your activities that take up 80% of your time and resources, you will be able to effectively meet your stakeholders' expectations. At this point you list the Primary and Other activities, respectively.

Column 2 estimates How Many of each activity must be performed to meet the needs of your stakeholders. How many top managers must you hire? How many disciplinary actions will you have to handle? How many pieces of paper will you have to file? Many managers say, "How am I supposed to know?" or "That's too much work!" There is one simple answer, in the form of a question, "If you don't know what needs to be done, how can you get it done?"

For the Primary Activities, you want these estimates to be as educated and documented as possible, based on what HR must do to enable XYZ, Inc. to produce, market, deliver and service 2,000,000 Widgets. For the Other Activities, all you need is the manager's or the subject matter expert's best guess. An analogy of this would be a hardware store inventory. For the primary items like refrigerators or lawn mowers, you want the most educated guesses possible, but for the other items like nails or paper clips, the subject matter expert's best guess is good enough. When you have completed columns 1 and 2 you have completed the forecast—The What and how many—and again there are *no* dollar signs. You continue with columns 3, 4 and 5, however, to determine the cost of meeting this forecast.

Columns 3 and 4 are how you arrived at the cost for each department in Step 4 of the organizational forecast. You first, in column 3, estimate the **Cost per Activity**, which is a similar process to determining the cost per unit in manufacturing. As an example, you determine, based on your past records and industry information, the average cost of hiring a top manager or the average cost of handling a disciplinary action or filing a piece of paper. Again, for the Primary Activities, you want documentation on your estimates, but for the Other Activities, the subject matter expert's best guess is good enough. You total these (the number of activities from column 2 times the cost per activity from column 3) and place the total in column 4. When you total column 4 it gives you the cost for the department, which was used in Step 4 of the organizational forecast. *Many managers believe that the column* *total is the department forecast, or even worse, the budget, but it isn't. Columns 1 and 2 are the forecast.* Column 4 is only the estimated cost of providing the deliverables. If this process is done realistically, the column 4 total should be very close to the budget total (budgeting will be discussed in the next chapter).

Column 5 is for **Outsourcing**. You determine the cost per activity of outsourcing applicable activities and compare it with the internal cost per activity to determine which will give you the best value added.

In summary, the forecast is the projected units of product/service to be delivered to the stakeholders. It includes The What, The Quality and The Quantity.

Key Point Review (answers on page 164)

1. The purpose of the forecast is to determine: a._____, b._____ and c._____ .

2. Primary activities are: _____.

3. Why is it important to know the geographic area?_____
   _____

4. Why do you use column 5, Outsourcing? _____
   _____

5. Isn't forecasting just forecasting the budget? Yes_____No_____ Explain _____
   _____

6. What happens to plans and budgets if the organization's forecast changes up or down? _____

7. Which number in Illustration III-3-1 is the real forecast?_____

8. Which two columns in Illustration III-3-2 make up the departmental forecast? _____ and_____

9. When developing a departmental forecast you must identify the deliverables, called activities, that will allow your organization to be able to meet _____.

10. What resource will provide you with a more in-depth understanding of forecasting?
    _____

Chapter 4:
Budgeting

Budgeting is a process of projecting **The How**, called Resources in project management, or what is necessary to meet the forecast. The Forecast determines **The What**, called **Scope** in project management, or the Product/Service. Many people mistakenly believe that for internal operations, forecasting and budgeting are the same. The focus of the budgeting process should be on the information it provides.

> **Note:** It is *incorrect* to say that a manager forecasts a budget; they project it. It may be grammatically correct, but in business, as outlined, they are two separate functions. To eliminate confusion, they must be treated separately. Managers need to project a forecast, The What, and they must project a budget, The How.

In Chapter 3 the process for generating departmental Forecasts was explained. Once the decision maker has completed the first two columns of the departmental forecast (see Illustration III-4-1), they can then proceed to develop a budget that will allow them to accomplish the activities in the forecasted quantities. The following outlines one method of budgeting, which has five parts: Staffing Needs, Operating Needs, Fixed Asset Needs, Miscellaneous Needs and Contingency Needs.

Departmental Forecast First Two Columns

What	How many
Primary	
Hiring	50
Performance reviews	300
Etc.	xxx
Other	
Filing	xxxx
Policies change	xx
Compliance	xxx
Etc.	xxxx

Illustration III-4-1

Staffing Needs identifies your most valuable assets, your employees. This need will be used to serve as a model for the process associated with all the needs. The simple form of this process is a spreadsheet in Excel® with four primary columns (see Illustration III-4-2): the Line Item, the What, the Why and the How Much. Placed into a formula, the What, Why and How Much become **Facts + Assumptions = Dollars**.

Budgeting spreadsheet

Staffing Needs

Item	What		Why		How Much
List all	Facts	+	Assumptions	=	$

Operational Needs

Item	What		Why		How Much
List all	Facts	+	Assumptions	=	$

Capital Needs

Item	What		Why		How Much
List all	Facts	+	Assumptions	=	$

Miscellaneous Needs

Item	What		Why		How Much
List all	Facts	+	Assumptions	=	$

Contingency Needs

Item	What		Why		How Much
List all	Facts	+	Assumptions	=	$

Illustration III-4-2

The *first step* is to determine and list all the staff necessary to perform the work. The decision maker needs to list all positions: full-time, part-time, ad hoc, outsourced and independent contractors. You may not obtain all of them, but when planning you must make sure to list all of them. This provides you with the information necessary to compensate for what you do not get.

The *second step* is to take each position one at a time and list all the facts under the What; for example, the manager of a Research and Development Department for a major drug company, assuming that it is a position that needs to be filled. To be considered a fact, the information must be supported and verifiable in writing. For this position, it would be reasonable to assume that this senior research scientist manager would be required to have a Ph.D. in the field; a number of certifications (for this example, 4); and a number of years of experience (for this example, 10). These requirements may come from a federal or state agency, from industry standards or from the organization's internal quality control standards.

Note: For some positions there may be no facts, only assumptions.

Once all the available facts have been listed, the decision maker can determine a salary range. For this example, it has been determined, from state and industry information and by talking to college placement departments, that the salary range is $90,000 to $140,000. Every year, the decision maker must revisit these facts to correct for any changes, called **Zero Based Budgeting**.

The *third step* is for the decision maker to identify and list all their assumptions. The Why refers to the assumptions, based on the facts, which determine their decisions about selecting a specific candidate. The decision maker starts by looking at all the facts related to each candidate. For this example, the candidate is Sandy. She has a qualifying Ph.D., 6 certifications and 12 years of experience and is currently making $88,000. All additional facts would be listed. The decision maker's first assumption may be that they want to fill the position for between $90,000 and $100,000, listing the reasons why. The next assumption is that Sandy is the right person and will accept the position for $95,000, listing the reasons why.

The *fourth step* is to insert the amount of $95,000 in the fourth column.

This process is repeated for each line item. In reality, this level of detail is limited to the primary line items as in the forecasting process. The summation of the line items results in the total budget. The problem is that after all this work, upper management wants you to cut it by 10%, which brings up the most important part of good budgeting. Good budgets are based on information, not numbers.

Question: Is line item "Sandy" $95,000, or is it a Ph.D., 6 certifications and 12 years of experience? People who want to believe that a budget is based on accounting say $95,000. This is wrong. Money cannot think or solve problems. You eat food, not money, and you cannot stuff money in your gas tank. Money is not a resource; it is only a medium of exchange. People, food and gasoline are the resources. If you need 100 gallons of gas to get to your destination, cutting it by 10% will leave you with a lot of walking. If line item "Sandy" was $95,000 and you cut it by 10%, which would be $9,500, that would reduce the salary to $85,500, which is $2,500 less than she is currently making and $4,500 less than a qualified person is willing to accept.

The **"Pad and Cut"** sickness of the 20th century has been replaced by Value Added, which is based on information, not just numbers. In addition, you cannot cut a fact or even an assumption by 10%. You can discuss them and modify them, but not just arbitrarily cut them. If you bring your manager a budget based just on dollars, they will probably cut it by 20% because they know that you have padded it by 10%.

> **Note:** Good budgeting, like good management, is a lot of hard work requiring training and practice. Because many managers lack proper training, they resort to budgeting based on dollars because it is easy. The manager, however, who uses real information to create budgets will be able to effectively negotiate for what they need.

This process is then repeated for each of the needs.

Operational Needs are all, except for staffing, operating expenses. This includes items like paper, rent, electricity and supplies. For each line item, Facts + Assumptions = Dollars.

Capital Needs are the Fixed Assets like buildings, vehicles and equipment. For each line item, Facts + Assumptions = Dollars.

Miscellaneous Needs are all additional known expenses, which are anticipated but not a normal expense. For each line item, Facts + Assumptions = Dollars.

Contingency Needs are for unknown events of the future. Chapter 6 will discuss the process for contingency planning. For each line item, Facts + Assumptions = Dollars.

> **Note:** This appears to be a lot of work. It is! Good decision making requires a lot of information, not just the manipulation of dollars. On the bright side, most of the line items do not change every year, so once you have created the basic budget, it becomes a powerful tool.

The information obtained from this process provides a base for creating all the financial (dollar) budgets that are used in business. Most budgets, when finished, resemble the Income Statement in appearance. The information is converted to dollars because it is the medium of exchange, but remember, the numbers are only as good as the information behind them: **Facts + Assumptions = Dollars**.

In summary, budgeting is not the manipulation of numbers; it is defining how the goal will be accomplished.

Key Point Review (answers on page 164)

1. Budgeting projects _____ .

2. In Project Management, the How is called _____ .

3. Budgets should be based on_____ , not dollars.

4. Should you ignore line items you do not believe you will receive? _____

5. A fact is something that can be _____ .

6. Assumptions are the decision maker's _____ .

7. Line item "Sandy" is_____ .

8. "Pad and Cut" is a _____ from the 20th century.

9. Proper _____budgeting is the basis for financial budgeting.

10. Budgeting is not the manipulation of numbers; it is the defining of_____ .

Chapter 5:
Project Management

Project Management is a process that allows large numbers of professionals, each doing different functions, to work together and effectively accomplish a goal. It is much like an orchestra within which different musicians can come together and present Chopin. Project Management is also an art form which works to modify the process to adapt it to the changing reality of the future, like a pilot adjusting a flight plan.

Too many managers either adhere dogmatically to the process or they ignore it. Good management is somewhere in between. This chapter focuses on the process, which incorporates your new understanding of accounting and financial processes. Chapter 6 will focus on the art of dealing with change and risk.

The Project Management Process is being developed in several different ways by industry organizations. The Project Management Institute **(PMI)** sponsors the Project Management Professional (PMP) certification. The Computing Technology Industry Association **(CompTIA)** sponsors the IT project and certification. This chapter is not going to restate what has been presented by them. It focuses on you, the non-financial manager, who may not be a formal project manager, but who still has a job to do and things to get done within time lines.

Life is management and in the 21st century, if an activity has deliverables and a due date, it is a **Project**. A **Process** is a project that is done repeatedly. Project Management is a function of three constraints: The What, The When and The How. These three constraints form a triangle, as shown in Illustration III-5-1.

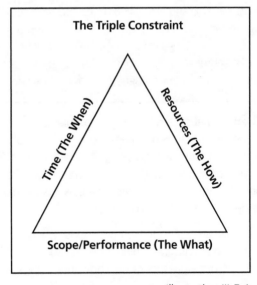

Illustration III-5-1

The What, called **Scope** or **Performance** in Project Management, is the desired outcome. In business it is the deliverables to the customer, called products/services, but it also includes internal customers like your boss. In government it includes "Putting a man on the Moon and bringing him back safely." For a family it includes preparing a Thanksgiving dinner.

The What represents the real bottom line; success or failure is based on customer satisfaction. In business the process for determining The What is called forecasting. For an in-depth understanding of forecasting, which defines The What, a college textbook on marketing is recommended. Your success is defined by your understanding of what must be done and the performance constraints associated with it.

The What may not be possible, at least in terms of desired outcome (**Features**), **Quality** and **Quantity**. Successful projects begin by clearly defining the performance constraints, divided into these three categories—features (deliverables), quality and quantity—and by asking questions that clarify the customer's expectations in these three areas. Examples: What if you just get them to the Moon safely? Times being so hard, will chicken be okay for Thanksgiving dinner? Are you willing to pay for a Cadillac? If we deliver 10 by Friday, will the end of the month be okay for the rest?

Until you have defined the Scope of the project in terms of features, quality and quantity, The When and The How are not relevant. It is true that The When and The How place constraints on The What, but they are still only functions of The What.

> **Note:** The What is and always has been the bottom line, called customer satisfaction. Yes, employees, owners, vendors, resources and time are important, but not one penny of revenue comes from them; 100% of all revenue comes from customers. In the 21st century the term Value Added means a resource's contribution to customer satisfaction, or when benefits provided exceed benefits consumed.

The When is what causes the biggest problems, because it is the future. The What is the bottom line, but The When is management. All too often the decision makers are all hung up on The What and The How without understanding The When. Besides, the customer wants it yesterday. Yes, many managers and customers try to make time a performance constraint; it is not. You cannot treat time as a performance constraint; in fact, most often, they are opposite. Haste makes waste!

Example: If you are willing to wait until Sunday, you can have a Turkey dinner, but if you insist on having Thanksgiving dinner on Thursday, it will have to be chicken. In addition, there are laws of nature that govern how long things take, like the drying of concrete, travel time, wrapping 5 packages—or 5,000,000.

Time is the future; it is a guess. And yet, people claim to be able to fix budgets. What is a budget really? A budget line item is simply the allocation of a resource over time. If your **Billable Rate** is $100 an hour and you are going to work for three hours, the budget line item is $300; if it takes you five hours, the budget line item becomes $500. The problem with general business budgets is that they are always for one year; the time period is fixed. This is not true in Project Management; the period may be 27 days or 18 months. If you waste an hour, you have wasted $100 worth of Value Added.

> ***Note:*** Estimating time and realistic time lines, understanding time constraints and knowing that all time estimates are guesses is one of the biggest keys to successful Project Management.

The How is the resources necessary to fulfill The What and accomplish the goal. Money is not a resource; it is only a medium of exchange. The resources are the people and physical assets necessary to perform the work. It is true that the lack of money may reduce the availability of resources, but it is still not a resource. The budget process defined in Chapter 4 must be used to determine the necessary resources and resource constraints. Sandy, not the $95,000, is the resource. You may get arguments from many people about this, but try to be polite when you point out their ignorance.

In summary, Project Management uses the accounting and financial information to support the development of good forecasts that clearly define The What (Scope/performance) and good budgets that define The How (resources) and to assist in effectively estimating The When (Time). The triangle for the Triple Constraints must always have its corners meet. Any and all changes in one area must be met with appropriate changes in one or both of the others. Remember all changes must result in customer satisfaction.

Key Point Review (answers on page 164)

1. Project Management is both a _____ and an_____ .

2. Too many managers either _____ or _____ the process.

3. A project is an activity that has a _____ and a _____ .

4. A process is a project that is done _____ .

5. Project Management has three constraints, which are: _____ , _____
   and_____ .

6. The What, which defines the deliverable, is the constraint called _____ .

7. The When, which causes the biggest problems, is the constraint called_____ .

8. The How, which outlines the process for getting it done, is the constraint called

   _____ .

9. The Forecast defines _____ .

10. The Budget defines _____ .

Chapter 6:
Change/Risk Management

Change/Risk Management deals with the real bottom line when it comes to management. If the future was known so that you could actually plan what would happen, there would be no need for managers; you could train a monkey to do it or program a computer. The future, however, is unknown; every plan is a guess and the only constant is change. The process for assessing and managing **Change** and **Risk** is called **Contingency Planning**.

What is Contingency Planning? It is having a spare tire in your car or carrying an umbrella. Contingency Planning in business is the highly skilled process of preparing for the uncertainty of the future. Is Contingency Planning new? No; it has been a part of the human survival process since the cave man devised defenses against wild animals.

The problem arises when modern business decision makers take things for granted and do not prepare proper Contingency Plans. **What if** there is a 9/11, a hurricane Katrina, a UPS or airline strike, a longshoremen's strike on the West Coast, a sick key employee, an oil embargo, a vendor who fails to deliver or we go to war? That list was just from the last ten years.

> **Note:** You cannot be hurt by what you are prepared to deal with; it is only the unexpected that can blindside you. The key is to expect that the unexpected will happen.

The future, the unknown and change represent the **#1 fear** of the human species. People (decision makers) fear the unknown and change because they are afraid that if something different happens, they may not be able to handle it, they may fail or they may be embarrassed. If change or fear of the unknown bothers you, do not accept a position as a manager. Good managers thrive on the challenges and opportunities that the uncertainty of the future provide.

In business, especially in businesses that are fixated on profits, the problem is that contingency planning costs money. Sometimes the cost of resources like smoke detectors, spare tires, umbrellas and even the training of staff is for events that will not happen.

Two factors affect the decision maker's response: Impact and Probability.

Impact is defined using the fifth spreadsheet in the budgeting process, which lists Contingency Needs. All possible events are listed, the facts stated, the assumptions made and an impact in dollars determined, if possible. This would be the ideal model, but time is of the essence and the number of possibilities is infinite. Also, things are constantly changing so the decision maker needs a process that they can develop into skill sets.

Probability is a mathematical guess; however, sometimes an event with even a very low probability that would have a high impact, like 9/11, must be properly prepared for. The same problem exists as did for impact. The probability for a given event is constantly changing. Again, the decision maker needs a process for identifying the probabilities that can be developed into skill sets.

The **Process** is called **Contingency Planning**. There are seven steps to this process (see Illustration III-6-1): Identify **Required Events**, identify impact events, estimate impact, estimate probability, plot estimates, identify action events and develop Contingency Plans.

Model for Contingency Planning

Events	Impact	Probability
1	High	Low
2	Low	High
3	Medium	Medium
4	High	High
5	High	Medium
6	Medium	High
7	High	High

Probability

High	A 2	B 6	C 4, 7
Medium	D	E 3	F 5
Low	G	H	I 1
Impact	Low	Medium	High

Contingency Plans are necessary for
Events: 6, 4, 7, 3 & 5

Illustration III-6-1

Identify Required Events: This is the Project Management Process which defines The What, The When and The How.

Identify Impact Events: This step answers the question **"What if?"** What if an employee gets sick or quits? What if there is a power failure? What if there is a tornado, a 9/11, a hurricane Katrina, a strike? All possible events that could impact business operations must be listed. They may have low probability or impact, but even very small events can cause big problems if you are not ready to deal with them.

Estimate the Impact: It would be nice if you could prepare a detailed **Facts + Assumptions = Dollars** analysis for every impact event; unfortunately that is just not possible. Therefore, you need a way to estimate the impact quickly that gives you reliable information. The process used in Illustration III-6-1 uses three categories: high impact, medium impact and low impact. Some models try to use only two categories: high and low. These models are hard to use because it is often difficult to define the line between high and low. The use of high, medium and low is effective because it assumes that the decision maker can sense the high and low items; the ones that they are not sure of are medium. This process, with practice, can be done quickly and reliably.

Estimate the Probability: The same three-category process is applied: high probability, medium probability and low probability.

Plot Estimates: Placing probability on the *y* axis and impact on the *x* axis, you plot all impact items.

*Identify **Action Items**:* These are the events found in sections B, C, E and F. They all have high and/or medium impact and probability.

There may be more, however. The items listed as low impact may change, especially if they have high probability. Example: An employee who has two unexcused absences in any quarter may be considered low impact, but five absences in one month is medium or even high impact. One small bump or pothole in the road will not hurt your car but a thousand could. The decision maker needs to identify all low impact items with breaking points, like 2 absences in a 90-day period is low, 3 to 8 is medium, 9 or more is high. This could create more action items that have Contingency Plans in place if the item exceeds the breaking point.

The same process is necessary for low probability/high impact items. Now the decision maker is looking for events, called triggers, that could move the item from low probability to medium or high. A better understanding can be obtained from courses and books on assessing and managing risk.

With this model, the decision maker can develop the skill sets that will allow them to very quickly, in the split second called the present, identify, classify and respond to unexpected events.

Develop Contingency Plans: Contingency Plans with **Contingency Funds** must be developed that will allow the organization to navigate successfully through life's changing storms to accomplish their desired goals.

> ***Note:*** Things will still occur that the decision maker has not prepared for; however, if they have mastered the skill sets, they will be able to spot the unexpected event a little sooner; classify it a little faster; and have existing contingency plans and funds to draw from, allowing them to effectively resolve the crisis.

In summary, **Change/Risk Management** is the real bottom line when it comes to management. If things went the way you planned, there would be no need for managers. Organizations survive by having managers trained in the art of problem solving through Contingency Planning that allows them to think on their feet and solve problems on the fly, in that split second called the present.

Key Point Review (answers on page 164)

1. The real bottom line for a successful manager is managing _____ and_____ .

2. Managing Change and Risk is called _____ .

3. A problem modern day managers have is_____ .

4. The future is _____ .

5. Change is the _____of the human species.

6. The problem with Contingency Planning is that it _____ .

7. Contingency Planning is necessary to identify the _____ .

8. Sometimes Contingency Planning means spending money for things you hope will _____ .

9. You cannot be hurt by what you have_____ .

10. You can only be blindsided by the _____

Chapter 7:
Key Points and Terms

Management is not controlling, it is guiding. Life cannot be controlled, only lived. To be successful, managers must understand the Lessons Learned and apply the knowledge to improving the **Best Practices**.

Planning creates the time line—the flight plan that the organization wishes to follow.

Contingency Planning tries to identify and prepare for all of the events that may prevent the organization from achieving its goal.

Controlling is an effort to phase the plan to Life's ever-changing uncertainty.

Management, therefore, is a process and an art. In the 21st century, the process is mastered by developing skill sets in Project Management and the art is developed through understanding how to assess and manage risk/change, called Contingency Planning.

Managers must master the three concepts which make up the Triple Constraint: The What, the How and the When.

The What, called Scope, is defined through the Forecasting process. It is what the customer, external or internal, wants. It is why the enterprise is undertaken. If it can be done in a way that the customer is ready, willing and able to pay for, there may be a business opportunity.

The How, called Resources, is defined through the budgeting process, which is not dollars but Facts plus Assumptions. It is Ph.D.s, buildings, pens and paper, which are the resources necessary to perform the work. If the How can be provided with Value Added, then there is an opportunity for a successful business.

The When, called Time, is the real key. The decision maker can plan until they are blue in the face, but if they do not have enough time it will not happen. All time management is a guess—it is the future. The past cannot be changed, the present is an instant and the future is unknown. Managers cannot control time; they can only phase their plans to it.

In conclusion, managers need to master the process so that they can effectively concentrate on the art of guiding their organizations through Life's mystery.

Key Terms:

#1 Fear – The number one fear of the human species is the fear of the unknown (change)

Action Items – The future events for which Contingency Plans should be prepared

Assumptions – The decision maker's educated guesses about the future

Best Practices – The educated guesses (laws, plans, decisions) for the future

Billable Rate – The hourly cost of consuming (using) a resource, normally employees

Breakeven – The level of sales at which marginal benefits equal marginal costs

Budgeting – The projection of how the resources will be deployed to accomplish the Forecast

Capital Needs – The spreadsheet in the budgeting process dealing with Fixed Assets

Change – The only true constant; managing change is the function of management

Change/Risk Management – The process of assessing change, risk and probability

CompTIA – Computing Technology Industry Association

Contingency Funds – Funds set aside to be deployed if a Contingency Plan is activated

Contingency Needs – The spreadsheet in the budgeting process that deals with the future

Contingency Planning – The process of preparing for the uncertainty of future changes

Controller – In the 21st century the Controller should be a provider of information to managers

Controlling – The real function of management; the process of phasing the plan to reality

Cost per Activity – The Cost Accounting process applied to activities

Departmental Forecasting – The Forecasting process brought down to the manager's functions

Dollars – The medium of monetary exchange used in the United States

Effectively – The process of **Efficiently** getting the right thing done

Efficiently – Getting it done fast and cheap, even though it may be wrong

Facts – Information about the past that can be documented and verified in writing

Features – The deliverables to the customer

Flight Plan – The project plan of a pilot

Forecasting – The process of projecting the units of product/service to be delivered to customers

Impact – The cost to the business of an unexpected event disrupting the operational process

Management – The process of modifying or phasing the plan to reality

Miscellaneous Needs – The spreadsheet in budgeting dealing with non-operational activities

Non-financial Manager – Any manager not working or trained in finance or accounting

Operational Needs – The spreadsheet in budgeting dealing with general operating resources

Organizational Forecasting – The identifying of product/service to be sold to customers

Outsourcing – The process of leasing staff and resources instead of hiring and purchasing them

Pad and Cut – The 20th century game of manipulating the budgeting process

Planning – The process of outlining how you will achieve your goals

Performance – Where you are in terms of where the customer needs you to be

PMI – The Project Management Institute; one of the primary Project Management Associations

Probability – The likelihood that a given event will occur

Process – A project that is done repeatedly

Project – An activity that has deliverables and a due date

Quality – One of the three defining characteristics of the performance constraint called Scope

Quantity – One of the three defining characteristics of the performance constraint called Scope

Required Events – The events essential to the successful fulfillment of the objective

Risk – The uncertainty associated with all future events

Scope – The Project Management term meaning the deliverables of a project

Staffing Needs – The spreadsheet in budgeting dealing with human resource needs

Target Market – The demographically defined customer base

The How – Refers to how the resources will be used to achieve the desired objectives

The What – Refers to the deliverables call Scope that will meet the customer's needs

The When – Refers to the time lines that define when the objective can be achieved

Time – The illusive function on the Triple Constraint used to schedule future events

Timely information – The best information available at the time it is needed

What if? – The primary question that every manager must continually ask about everything

Window of Opportunity – The best point in time to make a decision or to take action

Workable Market – The geographical area within which the business can be successful

Zero Based Budgeting – The reconfirming of Value Added for every line item each year

Appendix – Key Point Review Answers

Part I:

Chapter 1: 1. benefits provided; 2. benefits consumed; 3. net exchange of benefits; 4. benefits; 5. dollars; 6. more value today than yesterday?; 7. financial events; 8. dollars; 9. benefits; 10. financial statements

Chapter 2: 1. Assets, Liabilities, Owner's Equity, Revenue and Expenses; 2. future benefits at cost; 3. dollars owed/spent for future benefits; 4. claims of the creditors; 5. claims of the owners; 6. the equation must always be in balance and the total left-hand entries must always equal the total right-hand entries; 7. claims; 8. accounts; 9. T; 10. debit, credit

Chapter 3: 1. six; 2. activities that can be measured in dollars; 3. No; 4. General Journal; 5. General Ledger; 6. accounting staff; 7. Assets, Liabilities and Owner's Equity; 8. Revenue and Expenses; 9. Balance Sheet, Income Statement and Cash Flow Statement; 10. federal offense

Chapter 4: 1. future benefits and claims; 2. the future benefits at cost; 3. Liabilities and Owner's Equity; 4. x-ray; 5. Current Assets, Fixed Assets, Current Liabilities, Long-term Debt and Owner's Equity; 6. one year; 7. footnoted; 8. cost; 9. balance; 10. past profits reinvested for owners

Chapter 5: 1. Balance Sheets; 2. Matching Principle; 3. normal operations; 4. Net Income; 5. sale; 6. dollars earned/received for benefits provided; 7. dollars owed/paid for benefits consumed; 8. net exchange of benefits; 9. owners want to know what their shares earned; 10. benefits (value)

Chapter 6: 1. cash in and cash out; 2. circulating capital; 3. profit/loss, financial health; 4. out; 5. in; 6. in; 7. out; 8. Fixed Assets; 9. debt and equity; 10. Cash Flow Statement

Part II:

Chapter 1: 1. finance; 2. Leverage Ratio; 3. the investors want to get their money back; 4. Debt; 5. Factoring; 6. Capital; 7. Equity borrowing; 8. educated guesses; 9. Lessons Learned; 10. Best Practices

Chapter 2: 1. trends; 2. guessing; 3. accounting; 4. two numbers, ratio; 5. liquidity; 6. functionally bankrupt; 7. financial ratios; 8. transactions; 9. good decision making; 10. health

Chapter 3: 1. quantity or price; 2. seller's market; 3. single unit of sale; 4. more than one unit; 5. Profits; 6. cost of Equity capital; 7. forecasted units; 8. benefits, costs; 9. Value Added; 10. insights

Chapter 4: 1. future; 2. same time; 3. Time Line; 4. Forecast; 5. cash in; 6. growth mode; 7. little or no growth; 8. uncertainty; 9. Facts; 10. timing and probability

Chapter 5: 1. financial statements; 2. computer generated spreadsheet; 3. Forecast; 4. Forecasts and Budgets; 5. trap; 6. Balance Sheet and Cash Flow Statement; 7. Projected Cash Flow Statements; 8. cash flow; 9. a poor cash flow period for your customers; 10. The What, The How and The Why

Chapter 6: 1. Fixed Assets; 2. return the investment the quickest; 3. the time value of money; 4. discounts; 5. the investment; 6. positive; 7. estimated cash flows; 8. trial and error; 9. positive Net Present Value; 10. elusive

Part III:

Chapter 1: 1. modifying/phasing; 2. Planning; Contingency Planning and Controlling (guiding); 3. granted; 4. rational; 5. change, risk and probability; 6. normal things go wrong; 7. practice; 8. future; 9. the fear of the unknown; 10. Guiding

Chapter 2: 1. provides information to decision makers; 2. timely information; 3. the customer needs you to be; 4. window of opportunity; 5. decision maker needs; 6. the information; 7. will be used; 8. timely manner; 9. past; 10. future

Chapter 3: 1. The What, The When, The How; 2. the ones that consume the most time and dollars; 3. It defines the workable market; 4. To define whether doing it in-house or outsourcing would provide the best Value Added; 5. No, the Budget is the How, the Forecast is the What; 6. They must change as appropriate; 7. The number of units to be sold; 8. Columns 1 and 2; 9. expectations; 10. a good college textbook on marketing

Chapter 4: 1. The How; 2. Resources; 3. information; 4. No; 5. documented in writing; 6. best guesses; 7. Ph.D.; 6 certifications and 12 years' experience; 8. sickness; 9. informational; 10. The How

Chapter 5: 1. process, art form; 2. adhere dogmatically, ignore; 3. deliverable, due date; 4. repeatedly; 5. The What, The When, The How; 6. Scope; 7. Time; 8. Resources; 9. The What; 10. The How

Chapter 6: 1. Change, Risk; 2. Contingency Planning; 3. taking things for granted; 4. unknown; 5. #1 fear; 6. costs money; 7. action items; 8. never happen; 9. planned for; 10. unexpected